Praise for *Communicate Excellence*

"Amy's comprehensive approach will maximize your practice's last frontier—your front office team. From making a great first impression to proper communication for scheduling and handling difficult patients, she shows how to dramatically improve conversion rates, build your practice, and create raving fans in the process. Along the way, your staff will be learning valuable skills, improving their job satisfaction and motivation. Implementing her time-tested methods will help build teamwork and reap big profits for your practice!"

—John K. McGill, CPA, MBA, JD, president of John K. McGill & Company, McGill & Hill Group

"Amy addresses an underappreciated and often overlooked component of patient care. This book is a valuable resource for any office manager."

—Christopher S. Vara, MD, pediatric orthopedic surgeon

"Amy Demas is on a mission to uncover the truth and make it known! She is hardwired to take any process and engineer it into an easy-to-understand process that flows. In her book, Communicate Excellence, *she has done just that for professionals in any industry who rely on an impactful first impression. Hello … aren't we all at the mercy of a positive first impression? Amy's*

communication process is effective and efficient and provides efficacy to any organization that applies her genius. While Amy holds an MBA degree, she is actually a master of business. This is a must-read for you and everyone on your team."

—Nicole Greer, CEO and principal coach of Vibrant Coaching, Inc.

"As I began reading the first preliminary chapters of Communicate Excellence not sure what to expect, I was completely captured by [Amy Demas's] authentic sharing of exactly what makes the difference. As a coach, mentor, and influencer in my own companies, I found myself saying 'Amen, sister.'

"The amazing part of what [Amy has] so beautifully captured is that it's not new knowledge … our own clients, as well as just about anyone who has attended a customer service presentation, have heard the invitation to 'make a difference, be the instrument of change, and go the second mile' before. But after reading the truths in your chapters, expressed in such an elegantly simple flow of conversation, will people hear it and care? Will they care enough to go back to their workdays and colleagues and be the instruments of change? I think they will.

"As I continued reading, I began to mentally sift through my client list, thinking of so many of my practices that could benefit from reading this book and engaging [Amy's] services. Congratulations, my friend and colleague. I need to spend more time with you to refresh my soul.

"With great affection for you and admiration in the spirit of your words."

—Mary Beth Kirkpatrick, managing partner of Impact360 Consulting and president of Gaidge

"The day I walked into the orthodontist office with my oldest child and their appointment system had been computerized was the last day I visited that office. When my next child needed braces, we found a warm and professional practice where we felt like family and received amazing care. Amy understands the impact of that first impression and is the staff member that every front office needs. She shares her knowledge through her business, Communicate Excellence, and now in this book in a way that is direct and relatable. In a time when communication is often reduced to a texted word or picture, Amy reminds us of the importance and power of human connection to positively impact our businesses and our lives. Every office and businessperson, for that matter, needs her coaching. I can't help but think how much more successful businesses would be if everyone in the office had interpersonal training!"

—Terry Walters, best-selling author of Clean Food

"I worked with Amy for several years in corporate America. Over my twenty-five-year career, a handful of people have made a profound impression on me—Amy is one of those people. She brings her authentic self to everything she does at both work and play. She cares about people and excels at making businesses successful—and she deeply understands the connection between those two things. She has demonstrated it again in this book.

"In short, if I had to assemble a trusted leadership team to deliver a critical product, process, or project, Amy is one of the first calls I would make. Speaking from personal experience, with Amy in my corner, the effort would be a resounding success and we'd have a fantastic time getting there!"

—Dan Bohen, senior vice president of US Bank

"Amy presents a repeatable process that when implemented makes a big difference with communication. I recommend taking the time to read what she has to offer."

—Ted Klee, senior vice president of Schneider Electric

"I have known Amy and her husband, Don, for several years and have found them to be very uplifting, joy-filled colleagues. Amy has worked with our team for the last eighteen months to help us improve our front office communications and interactions with our patients and our referral sources. She is a masterful teacher and has established excellent rapport with our team and our doctors. She is professional, well prepared, and nonintimidating, and her message is totally appropriate. She measures and monitors her coaching extremely well and is trustworthy beyond reproach. I consider Amy an invaluable part of our team, and we are all better off with her on board."

—Dr. Henry Zaytoun Jr., Zaytoun Orthodontics

"The first time I met Amy Demas, I instantly knew I had encountered a transformational leader. If you are lucky, you meet a few of these rare individuals throughout your life who have the imagination, drive, commitment, and ability to lead by inspiring those around them.

"She is a passionate innovator and educator with an ability to lead, dedicated to inspiring doctors and team members to recognize their roles in the success of a practice. Take time to read Communicate Excellence and learn from her."

—Rita Bauer, speaker, trainer, and consultant on dental photography

"Amy's approach is systematic. Her emphasis is on creating excellent habits for everyone who speaks to your family of patients. She coaches first impressions that are natural and yes, real! When she visits your office, Amy makes your team's individual strengths effective and weaknesses irrelevant. Her training and development never stops. I encourage you to read Communicate Excellence."

—Dr. Robert Bray, former president of the American Association of Orthodontists (AAO)

"I have known Amy for many years: first as her children's orthodontist, then as a friend and spouse of an orthodontist who is a close personal friend, and now as an orthodontic consultant. This book is an opportunity for us to gain some insights from her vast experience in the banking industry, as the spouse of an orthodontist, and now as a consultant who has seen the good, the bad, and the ugly in numerous orthodontic practices. Sharing her experiences with us in the form of a book is a true blessing to orthodontics."

—Dr. Dave Paquette, Paquette Orthodontics

"Communications expert and dynamic coach Amy Demas has written a how-to book that is a must-read for every

healthcare doctor and team interested in taking their practice to the next level.

"The unique 'Huddle Up' section following each chapter provides healthcare teams a road map for incorporating the valuable ideas in the book into the workplace.

"I highly recommend this book."

—Dr. Keith Hilliard, DMD, orthodontist

"Amy was a breath of fresh air for our orthodontic team. Excellence in customer service has always been an essential component of our practice philosophy, and Amy shed light on a variety of new and existing areas upon which we could improve and enhance the entire patient experience while increasing new patient conversions. Most importantly, she did so in a way that made each of our staff members feel encouraged, empowered, and excited to implement all that we learned during our time together. I highly recommend that you read her book and help your staff communicate with excellence!"

—Drs. Rich and Tracie Resler, Resler Orthodontics

"It is evident in this book that Amy has the expertise to train you in the art of communication, especially in the service context. She gives a clear picture of what it takes to build and sustain your business through authentic relationships with your customers. This is a must-read if you are searching for the right concept to make a difference in your business."

—Pauline Wickens, author of *The Birthing Room*

"Amy has been an incredible part of the orthodontic consulting world, and I am especially impressed with her commitment to the profession and desire to help everyone improve. Not only are her ideas spot on but they are incredibly timely and valuable. I look forward to her Communicate Excellence e-mails, and with her enthusiastic permission, I have used her concepts in my own presentations and shared them with my own clients."

—Lynne Nickels, senior consultant at Impact360

"With this book Amy has condensed her innovation skills and interpersonal insights into actions that can transform a practice."

—James Heddleson, PhD, engineering science

"Amy Demas makes a compelling case for communicating warmth and care as much as quality deliverables—and she shows you how it's done!"

—Pastor Doug Falls, Stonebridge Church Community

"I own a tech company. Most of our contact with clients revolves around e-mails, instant messaging, and texts. It's far too easy to have accidental communication through these mediums where facts are conveyed back and forth but the intentional acts of listening, understanding, and responding are left behind. Amy and coaches like her have helped remind me about the importance of all communication and paying attention to the times my team and I have to refresh and strengthen the relationship we have with those we serve."

—Chet Cromer, president and CEO of C2IT Consulting

"I have had the pleasure of knowing Amy for more than a decade: first through her husband's orthodontic practice and more recently through her orthodontic consulting. She has always been forward thinking and persistent in ensuring processes are the best they can be. I am excited to see Amy sharing her knowledge through this book. She truly practices what she teaches, and everyone can benefit from her understanding of customer service and communication."

—Amy Schmidt, president of Ortho2

What Amy's Clients Are Saying

"[Amy] restored the confidence in my receptionist as to how to take control of the phone call."

—Ann, office manager of Thomas Orthodontics

"[Having Amy as a coach helped] improve what you can't be there to improve."

—Dr. Allison Hamada, Hamada Orthodontics

"We have had four consultants work on different aspects of our practice. Most provided general comments on all aspects of the business. It was like sitting in an auditorium for hours, then going home and saying, 'That was a great lecture.' Then nothing changed. Nothing happened. When we hired Amy, it was all action! In fact, after she worked with us, we asked her for some specialized help with one of our team members, and she designed a program for her that has had a huge impact on her effectiveness in the business. No one felt put down or inadequate; it was all congenial yet targeted. I am excited for what she has done and is continuing to do for our already awesome team!"

—Dr. Kent Floreani, director of Azure Medispa; owner of Headlines Hair and Day Spa; Dr. Floreani, O'Toole & Dool Orthodontists; Great Lakes Honda; and Our Driving School

"When I was hired, I was new to the orthodontic field. Amy changed that. With her guidance and the resources that she provided, I quickly mastered the front desk position. Amy's instruction made me feel empowered. She had an extreme amount of patience not just in correcting anything I did wrong but also in showing me why it was wrong and providing me with the tools to do it correctly. She helped me thrive in my new role and made me confident and relaxed, which has made all the difference."

—Christie, treatment coordinator at Clauss Orthodontics

"Our experience with Amy's program has been a very positive and smooth process from the initial sign-up and orientation to the review of our needs, preparation for an office visit, and the on-site content and continued coaching. Amy's on-site presentation sought to reach out and understand each staff member's personality and their perspectives of their roles in our office organization. Her savvy understanding of what goes on in the front office reception area with phone calls as well as new patient processes had the staff realizing she sympathized with them and knew their challenges and rewards, and they warmly welcomed her approach to help them work through day-to-day scenarios. Amy is an excellent communicator, readily recognizes a practice's communication issues and needs, and works with and coaches individual staff members to help them perform at their peak!"

—Dr. Michael Mayhew, OP Smiles

"I have been to many different trainings and seminars, and Amy's was—by far—the best!"

—Jessica, treatment coordinator at Carr Orthodontics

"I would recommend [Amy's] program to all practices (not just orthodontics) who want to learn how to improve their customer relations skills!

"Amy is a wonderful authority and resource for our practice. Her insights into providing the highest level of customer service while running a busy practice with a high level of productivity are invaluable. Our team enjoyed her on-site workshop and has found her follow-up training sessions to be very organized, thorough, and practical. The work that she does listening to our admin team's phone calls and giving them feedback has changed the way we view each and every phone call. Her presentation style is relatable and engaging. She effortlessly helped our team come around to the right conclusions about the slight nuances and changes that they could make to improve their customer service with patients on a daily basis. We would invite Amy back again and again!"

—Anna, office manager at Saddle Creek Orthodontics

"I have known Amy for over ten years, and she is as solid a friend as you could hope for. She won't tell you, but she has over fifty-five patents in the financial industry and is now bringing her expertise to orthodontics. Amy is that rare person who understands the numbers completely, but her real value to your practice is her interpersonal skills. She will help you formulate your goals, then distill them to an 'elevator talk' and get your team completely on board to help you achieve goals beyond what you can currently conceive. If you're looking to move past your status quo

and want help navigating the changes in orthodontics, Amy is your guide. You can't go wrong."

—Dr. Lou Chmura, Chmura Orthodontics

"I have been in orthodontics for thirty-nine years and have sat through many seminars, and I found Amy's presentation to be one of my top three favorites!"

—Dianne, treatment coordinator at OP Smiles

"Amy's extensive background in engineering, business, leadership, and orthodontics help make her a tremendous coach and advocate for your practice. She is extremely organized, thoughtful, creative, and kind. I highly recommend her services."

—Dr. Kyle Fagala, Saddle Creek Orthodontics

"Our team has greatly benefited from Amy's training and coaching. She has helped us fine-tune the skills necessary to maximize interactions with both new and existing patients. Her coaching sessions are presented in a positive and encouraging manner that has been especially beneficial in how our current patients are scheduled, as well as in our approach to handling new patient phone calls. Amy has shown us the tremendous value of efficient and streamlined communication methods to assist in maximizing our practice's goals. I would highly recommend her training and coaching program to any practice looking to enhance their patient communication!"

—Dr. Lance Miller, Elevate Orthodontics Podcast

Communicate
Excellence

Communicate
Excellence

A GUIDE TO AUTHENTIC, POSITIVE, CONSISTENT FRONT DESK COMMUNICATION

AMY DEMAS, MBA, DTM, DFSS

Published by Advantage, Charleston, South Carolina.
Member of Advantage Media Group.

ADVANTAGE is a registered trademark, and the Advantage colophon is a trademark of Advantage Media Group, Inc.

Printed in the United States of America.

10 9 8 7 6 5 4 3 2 1

ISBN: 978-1-64225-126-5
LCCN: 2019918648

Cover design by James Earley.
Layout design by James Earley.

Front cover photo of Amanda Crowley of Weaver Orthodontics.
Front cover photo by Ingenuity Marketing.

This publication is designed to provide accurate and authoritative information in regard to the subject matter covered. It is sold with the understanding that the publisher is not engaged in rendering legal, accounting, or other professional services. If legal advice or other expert assistance is required, the services of a competent professional person should be sought.

Advantage Media Group is proud to be a part of the Tree Neutral® program. Tree Neutral offsets the number of trees consumed in the production and printing of this book by taking proactive steps such as planting trees in direct proportion to the number of trees used to print books. To learn more about Tree Neutral, please visit **www.treeneutral.com**.

Advantage Media Group is a publisher of business, self-improvement, and professional development books and online learning. We help entrepreneurs, business leaders, and professionals share their Stories, Passion, and Knowledge to help others Learn & Grow. Do you have a manuscript or book idea that you would like us to consider for publishing? Please visit **advantagefamily.com** or call **1.866.775.1696**.

Dedication

To Don. You are my water and wind, ever encouraging me to step out of my comfort zone and make an impact. I love you.

To Mom. Where would I be without you? From infancy to adulthood, you have always been there. From tears to cheers, you upheld me. I love you.

To Nicole. You are my life coach who saw my possibilities and held me accountable to make them probable. Thank you.

Table of Contents

Foreword

Communicate Excellence: A Guide to Authentic, Positive, Consistent Front Desk Communication is a truly insightful book. The author uses her background in process analytics to tease apart the critical aspects of the front desk position. Using quotes from people such as Aristotle to Dr. Robert Cialdini while detailing the polite nature of a persuasive conversation, Amy's emotional intelligence helps provide "aha!" moments for the reader.

Amy Demas has successfully copatented, with Bank of America, more than fifty-five patents related to process. Her understanding of statistics-driven success allows the reader to look inside her thoughts and see step-by-step, practical messages that help guide the reader through the new patient enrollment process.

I am impressed with the way her use of phraseology can clarify the entry process. *Communicate Excellence* teaches, depending on personality type and situation, when it is appropriate to speak in single sentences or entire paragraphs.

In most cultures, the term *teacher* is the highest possible compliment a person can receive. Amy Demas is both a teacher and a coach because of her native abilities to communicate effectively.

Please enjoy *Communicating Excellence*. I'm certain you will find your own "aha!" moments.

W. Ronald Redmond, DDS, MS, FACD
CEO emeritus, Schulman Group

Introduction

YOU HAD ME AT HELLO

We had just moved from South Carolina to the Charlotte, North Carolina, area, and I needed to find a new dentist for my kids. At the time, they were around ages seven, nine, and eleven. Since we were so new to the area, I didn't know where in the world to go, and I really didn't have anyone to ask. I heard an advertisement on the radio for a local dentistry, so I decided to give them a try.

The practice was a two-story building, a sort of mega office with maybe thirty or more clinical bays for treatment. We walked up to the second floor and were met by a grandmotherly woman with the most amazing southern charm. She greeted me with "Miss Amy, I am so glad to see you" and then turned to my eldest and asked, "And you are?" After he replied, "Jesse," she then turned to my other children and, referring to them by name, said, "Oh, and Katy. Look at those angel kisses. And David, you must have a really neat big brother."

Now, I knew she had my name and my children's names in a computer, so she had a cheat sheet. But she used the power of deduction to ask my oldest child his name, and that helped her figure out who each of my other children were. By acknowledging them in such a lovely way—calling them by name, talking about their adorable freckles (angel kisses), and just generally loving up on them—she met my great needs as a mom.

She showed us to the waiting area, where I decided to sit strategically to observe her to see whether this experience was a show for first timers or her authentic self. What I saw was this: it didn't matter who came in or left. She knew every name and had something good to say: "Oh, my goodness, I loved seeing you" or "Bye now. We'll see you in six months." She made everyone she encountered feel welcome and special.

And that was the case year after year. She was the same genuine, incredible person every time we saw her. Here's the thing: it was such a big practice that we rarely saw the same hygienist—or the same doctor. The clinical care at that practice wasn't really a personal experience. But because of Tracy, we stayed. In other words, she really had me at hello.

In fact, Tracy was so impactful that her legacy spanned several states. When I was telling this story during a training session in New Jersey, someone in the room said, "By chance, is the person's name Tracy?"

The bottom line is if you can have a Tracy at your front desk, your clients are sold—and you're golden.

Training for First Impressions—Not Just an Afterthought

How many times have you called a medical office or any type of office and not even been able to get someone to say hello in a way that made you feel like they cared you were there? Even if you already know the doctor or the person you're trying to reach, you still have to persevere through the front desk. If you don't know the doctor, then how long are you going to put up with someone who is unfriendly and unhelpful—someone who doesn't seem to care?

The people at the front desk are your practice's ambassadors. Whether in person or on the phone, your receptionists and schedule coordinators create the first impression for the entire office. They set the tone for the experience anyone interacting with your office will have.

Think about the impact of a receptionist who doesn't seem to care if your office provides complimentary consultations. Patients have options—they can go to multiple providers for free consultations; they can go to any provider for care. That's why first impressions are so important. The first impression is what sells you.

For orthodontic practices, plastic surgery offices, day spas offering cosmetic procedures, and other similar practices, front desk training and coaching in communications is usually an afterthought even though these types of places require higher out-of-pocket expenses from their clientele and patients' discretionary dollars. The clinical areas of these offices are required to go through different levels of training and certification. It's the same with treatment or patient flow coordinators, people who deal with sales and financing—they also tend to go through very thorough training.

But training for the people who create the first impression—the front desk, the scheduling coordinators, the receptionists—is often a matter of being provided date entry forms for first inquiry calls and maybe a book of scripts.

Then follow that up with the fact that feedback typically comes more in the form of scolding than empowerment. They're not equipped as to how to listen and respond; they're not taught proper mental posture or basic business principles. They are only evaluated maybe once a quarter when someone calls in, pretending to be a patient or client, to see how they answer the call. No one takes the time to teach them repeatable habits that can elevate every single encounter.

That's where I come in.

Been in Those Shoes

As a communications trainer and coach, I want to make sure that the first phone impression someone has with your business and the first physical impression align with each other. I bring training to the space that is usually an afterthought or gets minor attention.

While the path that brought me where I am today is not a straight line, at my core, I'm a coach and teacher. It's in my DNA. I come from a family of teachers—grandparents, a parent, and numerous siblings and cousins have been coaches or teachers. No matter where life and work have placed me, that truth comes out. I'm someone who likes to work on processes and gain feedback to make things repeatable.

I've also worked every administrative role in my husband's orthodontics office, which has helped me gain practical insight into best practices that I now use in coaching and training.

These experiences, and more, led to me becoming the founder and president of Communicate Excellence, a training and coaching program for your team.

My practical experience and perspectives help set apart my programs at Communicate Excellence. Since I've been in those shoes, I am able to do more than just theorize how a program or process should work; I actually know how to apply it to real-world situations. I bring the business and process skills into what have historically been very siloed roles. But I also know what it means to be on the other side of the desk or phone since it wasn't that long ago that I was a single mom with no dental or medical IQ and with a child needing braces.

Seeing things from diametrically opposed positions is something I've done my whole life. I've been single and married. Without kids and with kids. I've experienced both public school and homeschooling for my children. I've worked in the corporate world and in private practice. I've been a patient and customer. I've been behind and in front of the desk.

The tipping point for building my coaching firm, Communicate Excellence, came when I was diagnosed with cancer while I was still working at my husband's practice. I was unable to work during recovery, so I had plenty of time to think about what to do with the rest of my life. As a teacher at heart, I decided that what I do best is share what I know and make it possible for others to be better at what they do.

I love seeing the light bulb go on for people. It's amazing—and so satisfying—to see people make their own discoveries once they truly understand new information and how it will impact their jobs and their lives. I am always an upholder. That doesn't mean always being nice and never pointing out what can be improved, but it does mean empowering those on your team. From the first impression to a lasting impression, I'm going to share with you the secrets I've learned throughout my career on how your business can sell its

> I am always an upholder. That doesn't mean always being nice and never pointing out what can be improved, but it does mean empowering those on your team.

services. I want to make sure that not only that first impression is good but that we sustain it through the entire life cycle of your customer. What's important is that communication and interactions are authentic.

As part of my coaching approach, I have my students focus on one or two changes at a time. At the end of each chapter in this book, I'll give you a list of action items to consider. But I want you to choose one and focus on that as a way of making impactful change.

Through the assimilation of various business truths and applying them with real-world use in a business like yours, I've improved call flow and scheduling for countless companies. The result? More lucrative, thriving businesses and happier cultures in general.

Successful outcomes are impossible if you're just throwing a book of scripts at the front desk—it's through live coaching, observation, and concentration on small repeatable habits that thorough understanding is reached and behaviors are changed.

Let me show you how it's all done.

Part I

The Foundations

In this section, we'll discuss the foundational components for developing a team that creates a memorable journey for your customer. Whether it's on the phone or in your office, we'll discuss the basics of what it takes to keep a customer coming back—and enjoying their journey all along the way. I want you to understand how the entire brand experience matters, beginning with the first interaction on the phone and continuing on through every appointment to the final "till we meet again."

Chapter 1

The Experience

IT'S NOT JUST WHAT WE SAY THAT HELPS PEOPLE TO MAKE UP THEIR MINDS. ... IT'S EVERYTHING WE DO.

—BERNADETTE JIWA

Anyone who has traveled on a commercial airline knows about the "dreaded middle." What I'm talking about, of course, is sitting in the middle seat on a flight to your destination. The middle seat is a different experience altogether than sitting in a window or aisle seat. In the middle, you're squeezed between two other people for the duration, playing elbow tag for an armrest, with no way to negotiate for more legroom, and nothing in the way of a view except the back of the seat in front of you—never mind getting up at any point in the flight to retrieve a bag from overhead or to make a trip to the lovely lavatory.

Yet only a few inches to the left or right—in the window or aisle seat—the experience is completely different. On one side, you can gaze out at the clouds and control the window shade, and on the other, you can stretch your legs or more easily move freely about the cabin without having to first disrupt anyone else in your row. And when you include the option to pay for the Plus section, you get six extra inches of legroom—it's great! Either way, just a little more comfort can make a flight feel a lot more bearable.

The point is people are willing to pay for that little bit of extra comfort—even if it's for a relatively short period of time.

Yet the last time I checked, the person sitting in the middle seat arrives at the destination at the same time as someone sitting in a window or aisle seat or in another class of service.

There's something special about an experience that consumers are willing to pay for. Whatever the product or service, people will continue to come to you and refer to you if they find *an experience* that exceeds the ordinary. The experience is why Southwest has a loyal following—its fans keep the airline flying because of how they're treated by the people who work for the company, and it's why people will pay extra for an end seat. Experience is why people flock to Apple for its iPhones—it's not necessarily all about the quality of the product; it's about *the experience* of being part of the Apple community. In fact, Apple has made such a name for itself that it's practically immune to price pressure.

> Whatever the product or service, people will continue to come to you and refer to you if they find *an experience* that exceeds the ordinary.

Great Results *and* a Great Journey

In a world where self-pay professional services are increasingly competing against low-cost and/or direct-to-consumer products, there's something to be said for creating a great experience. Whether it's orthodontics, a plastic surgery procedure, treatment at a day spa, or some other professional service, people paying discretionary dollars want to know that they are more than just a number. They want their arrival to be anticipated and their experience to be curated for them personally. People are willing to pay more for great results, but they expect a great experience while receiving your service or obtaining your product. They're not paying only for expertise; they also want to enjoy the journey.

Sure, many consumers are looking for the cheapest product or service. Take the clear aligner market. With the direct-to-consumer option, the patient takes their own mold of their teeth, sends it in, and gets a set of aligners in return. But who's overseeing the treatment? Those people view a smile as a commodity. They think it doesn't matter where they go for treatment because they can get their teeth straightened anyway.

But plenty of parents still want the best for their kids, and many adults still want to be treated as special. These people know that a great smile—a great look—is more than a commodity.

Yet all the quality treatment in the world can't overcome a poor experience, especially at the front desk. If you are providing the best clinical treatment around, then the experience at your front desk should mirror that. Think about your own experiences: If you were to enter an office that felt dim and dull, would you want to be treated there? If you were greeted by grumpy, unhappy people at the front desk, why would you expect a better clinical experience?

The Softer Side—Measured by "Happier"

Experience is something that is felt by your consumers. It's something addressed by the softer side of your business or how you communicate with your consumers.

The softer side is harder to define, but you know it's there. You can feel it when you walk into an office—if there's tension in the room, you know it. More than obvious gossiping or backbiting, there are often subtle and even unseen signals that something's not quite right—a stealth rolling of the eyes, a slight smirk when reporting "doctor's running late—*again*." The manner in which your front desk treats customers gives them a sense of whether their needs are being put first.

On the other hand, if there's great energy in the room, you can feel that too. You can tell when a team is unified in message and action and policy. You can tell when they are authentically putting the needs of the customer first.

The softer side is all about how you connect with your customers—how you make people feel, how you meet and greet people every single time they come in. And it's driven by your internal culture.

Take a company such as the Ritz-Carlton, for instance. The Ritz-Carlton is known for its exceptional experience, one that has bred a loyal following of customers who willingly pay more for a room and expect more in return. How does it continually deliver more? Internal culture. The Ritz-Carlton is a company that sets expectations and articulates what it defines as successful behaviors to its team. It goes to great lengths to create a culture where people who work for the company *want* and are empowered to take care of guests.

> That's what people expect when they call your office with an issue—they expect a resolution, not excuses.

A team with a great internal culture is one that also knows how to handle "oops" moments. That's what people expect when they call your office with an issue—they expect a resolution, not excuses. Think about the last time a company handled an oops moment for you—did they find a way to make the problem right, or did they just dance around the issue?

Soft results can be hard to measure, but they ooze out everywhere. You know your customers are happier, and you know when your team is happier, but how do you quantify that?

With customers, the goal is to create raving fans. People never love their airlines, but they love Southwest. Why? Again, it's the experience. If people are happier about their experience with you, they will become your spokespeople. I'm an example of that. I love my Peloton bike. I tell people about it, I take pictures of it, I post it on my Facebook page. Recently, some of the live online classes Peloton offers went down, and when I reached out to the company, no one made excuses. They apologized to me and then, because it was impacting even more people, they made the extra effort to broadcast messages that gave continual updates as to the resolution of the issue. They went above and beyond and, in me, created a raving fan.

Raving fans will bring other people to your practice and create a sense of perpetual motion—they'll do some of your marketing footwork for you.

In staff, soft results are evident in increased confidence and reduced stress. When you have team members at your front desk who are trained and skilled in providing a great experience, they exude confidence when they represent you. You can hear it on the phone, and you can see it in person. You'll see it in the way your people respond to questions. When asked, "Do you have open hours on Friday?" instead of justifying or rambling on, "Um, no, we're not open on Fridays because, like, we do this or we do that," you'll hear your people confidently say, "We are currently seeing patients Monday through Thursday" and move on. They won't cower or make apologies for the way things are. They won't feel like they have to make excuses, and they won't have to defer to a manager for answers and resolution.

Training, Coaching—the Difference Makers

Creating a great experience is about standardizing your approach. It's easy to think "there's nothing to it" when it comes to staffing the front desk. Just tell them how to take the phone off night mode and answer when it rings. They know the greeting. How hard can it be?

Well, it is hard to create a unified first impression without a standardized approach. When you go into Crate & Barrel or L.L. Bean or an Apple Store, you know you're going to get a higher-quality experience. That's because those companies have a standardized approach. They train their people in culture, policy, and service—all the things they need to know to consistently create the right impression.

Without a standardized approach, you're leaving your front desk people to wing it, to go rogue. When you do that, each person is going to take from their own experiences—or lack of experience—and interpret their role and every situation in their own fashion. That's not to say that they don't have good intentions, but a lot of times this is the first professional, customer-facing role for these individuals. Sometimes it's their first job ever. Up to this point, communication skills for the youngest members of your team have likely been in text mode, and they've really never been shown how to talk professionally on the phone or one on one. They don't know how to talk to clientele and customers who have grown up on the phone or having face-to-face conversations. On the flip side are those older team members who are stuck in a that's-not-the-way-we've-always-done-it rut. These individuals sometimes have trouble realizing that the consumer of today is not like those consumers they knew when they entered the workforce. Whatever generation the members of your team belong to, they need to know how to talk on the phone to today's consumers and to do it in a professional way.

Through training and coaching, your team will become more knowledgeable about your products and services and also more in sync with their teammates. No more frustration from experienced senior team members who feel like they always have to cover for an untrained newbie—that kind of environment breaks trust in team members and in consumers coming to you. When you have a trained and coached team, you have a group of people working together to create a consistently great experience.

The more everyone in your practice is on the same page, the greater the sense of pride in the company. Once your team starts to gel, becoming one in mind and thought and actions, they start to have a sense of pride about you and their workplace. Now you've got a place where people want to work, a place that people don't want to leave—they would never consider going to work at a low-performing company or somewhere that does not have the same feel-good culture. The workplace becomes a safe zone, a place where team members have each other's backs. Instead of team members opposing or undercutting each other, everyone echoes the same sentiments. There are no "good cop, bad cop" situations because everyone holds the line when it comes to policy and procedure.

As an added bonus, your practice becomes a place that your team is proud to promote. They become your ambassadors and are glad to say, "Yes, I work there. You should come see us. We are the best."

Training and coaching also helps reveal which members of the team are not up to the task and have no desire to become so. If you never provide the training, you're never quite sure where the problem lies with team members who just don't seem to be up to their roles. Is it because they aren't willing or because they aren't able? If you provide the training and they still don't apply it, then you know what you need to do.

As I mentioned in the introduction, my mission is to uncover truths, to find those nuggets that will best empower your team. That's why, as part of my coaching, I sit at the table with your team as a mentor. I want to help your team sell from the first impression and then create a lasting impression throughout the life cycle of your customer—and beyond.

Creating a great experience does not happen by chance. We need a plan—a plan that can be implemented and that will yield the same results each time we have a new team member. In the chapters ahead, I'll share with you some insights about how this is done.

Huddle Up

As part of my coaching approach, I ask that you focus on one or two ways to improve at a time. At the end of each chapter, I'll give you a list of questions for reflection. Choose one and focus on it before moving ahead.

o   Think about a company or brand that has the most impactful impression on you. Is there something you can name about that experience that made it so?

o   Think about an experience that really turns you off. Why is that the case?

o   What have you done to create your own brand experience? Have you systemized it and trained to it?

Chapter 2

Plans Work

WE ARE WHAT WE REPEATEDLY
DO. EXCELLENCE, THEN, IS NOT
AN ACT, BUT A HABIT.

—ARISTOTLE

Would you ever try to build a skyscraper without following a blueprint? How confident would you be working on the top floor of such a building if you knew its construction crew had not followed a carefully designed plan? What about flying? Would you want to go up in a commercial jet if you knew its maintenance had not been done according to plan? If you knew the pilot had not followed the preflight checklist? Would you want to go into surgery knowing the team had not followed a presurgery and postsurgery checklist?

There are plenty of jobs that revolve around planning and checklists where people do their training according to such. Why? Because you want the job done right. Without a plan and training to that plan, all your callers, potential customers, and customers will hear is a lot of blah, blah, blah.

A good communications plan works because it is more than just a book of scripts for the front desk to robotically read off. It involves systematic training to change and build habits, to equip your team to consistently provide good customer experience. Everyone on the team needs to understand their role and what's expected of them. They must practice and rehearse what to say until it sounds natural and essentially becomes second nature. We want them to easily and quickly find that sweet spot where they're providing enough information to demonstrate appropriate knowledge while being brief enough that all the information can be absorbed. It's a tenuous tightrope.

The best way to stay on topic appropriately is to follow a defined plan. That plan can be an outline of what to cover at what level of detail. Or it can be a fully scripted monologue. The key is to not wing it.

As part of my coaching, I listen to over ten thousand calls every year. And what I've found is that if we execute certain repeatable steps in a consistent fashion, the whole experience of the conversation is elevated. Without a plan, team members tend to ramble or omit critical details. But when we plan for different scenarios and train to be adaptable, we foster the environment of a good experience.

A communications plan breaks down into repeatable habits. Without repeatable habits, there is simply too much to try to remember. It works bit by bit, one or two habits at a time. We don't just throw the book at staff—the book of scripts, that is—and expect them to get it.

Think about New Year's Day, one of the biggest habit days we have. We're all out there making our resolutions like we can just magically change overnight and forever. But let's face it: by the second week of January, and especially into February, most of us have already thrown up our hands and said, "Well, better luck next year."

It's not easy to change a habit. It requires discipline. And we're doing all this planning and training while still taking care of customers and patients. It would be great if we could be like one of those reality shows, like *The Biggest Loser*, and just head off to camp for several months while we work on our new habits. But it doesn't work that way. That's why we systematically only work on one, two, or maybe three habits at a time. That keeps us from being overwhelmed while continuing to enhance the customer experience.

Because with too much stress, we tend to regress and resort to the way we've always done things. It's like wearing retainers after braces. Teeth want to shift back to where they used to be. Habits are like grooves in a well-worn path. Our minds want to stay in those grooves because we know them so well; they're easy. And getting out of a groove can take some real effort. Imagine a horse trying to pull a wagon out of a groove—it pulls the wagon up, only to have it slide back down. Up, then down, up, then down. And once out of the groove, it's a little scary because there's no clear path ahead. But with systematic practice, we can create a new habit groove. Then by building habit upon habit, small change upon small change, we'll see great things happen.

> Habits are like grooves in a well-worn path. Our minds want to stay in those grooves because we know them so well; they're easy.

A Finite Life Cycle

In industries such as orthodontics and plastic surgery, the consumer life cycle is somewhat finite. While plastic surgery patients may come in for more than one procedure, in orthodontics there is generally a two-year life cycle to treatment. You're constantly looking to attract new customers. If you're going to capture patients and keep them for the comparatively short period of time that they are going to be with you, then you need to understand that customer experience is not an extra nice thing to offer but the gateway to get into the game. When customers are paying significantly out of their own pocket, they expect something special in return. Without that extra level of service, they'll go to other providers until they find what they're looking for—someone who meets their expectations.

If you're in the business of continually fighting for discretionary dollars, you need a plan, and you need to train to that plan.

That starts by understanding the foundation of the consumer life cycle, what's known as the "Moments of Truth."

Moments of Truth

The Moments of Truth concept looks at the critical milestones in the customer's or potential customer's journey—the opportunities where your team is able to engage with the customer and earn their business. A moment of truth is an experience that helps lock in an emotion to the brand. It helps shape and establish the impression customers have to the brand or the company.

> A moment of truth is an experience that helps lock in an emotion to the brand.

Moments of Truth

Stimulus	Zero	First	Second	Ultimate
Moment of Truth	Moment of Truth	Moment of Truth	Moment of Truth	Moment of Truth
Aware	Search	Contact / Purchase	Experience	Share

Fig. 2.1. Moments of Truth

The concept of "Moments of Truth" was originally developed by Procter & Gamble in 2005 as two moments: the first being when the customer initially comes in contact with your company or product and sometimes makes a purchase and the second being when they experience your product. Since the first two moments were formulated, Google has added the "Zero Moment of Truth"—the point in the customer journey when they begin searching for information about a product or service. The "Stimulus Moment of Truth," also known as the "Less Than Zero Moment of Truth," was then coined by Eventricity, and it marks the point in the journey when the customer first becomes aware of a product. Procter & Gamble later added the "Ultimate Moment of Truth" to the concept as the point in the journey when customers provide feedback.[1]

---

1   Matthew Draper, "What Are the Five Moments of Truth in Marketing?," Liferay, November 9, 2017, accessed June 24, 2019, https://www.liferay.com/blog/en-us/customer-experience/what-are-the-five-moments-of-truth-in-marketing-.

While these moments vary by company and consumer journey, what's important to understand is that they are ultimately about a great customer experience.

For example, with orthodontic or plastic surgery practices, consumers typically start their journey with an aha moment. That's the moment when they notice that their teeth are crooked or their tummy is hanging over their belt, and so they seek out your brand for help. Typically, through marketing or word of mouth, they've heard about your brand, so they may already have an idea that they want to make contact. But in a world where consumers often go through three or four consults before making a decision, how do you stand out?

That's where training to create a great experience comes in. In that first moment of truth, that first contact, it's crucial that the potential customer has a great experience. Usually, that first contact is a phone call, so it's important that the call goes well and that the person on the other end of the phone (in your practice) knows how to create the best impression.

What's different in an orthodontic or plastic surgery practice, day spa, or other similar business compared to those where the contact and purchase are made at the same time—like buying Pampers at Walmart—is that the moments of truth are spread out. There is often some lag time between the initial phone call and the decision to buy. That decision usually isn't made until after the customer comes in for a consultation. That's when you ask them to move forward with treatment. Plus, since your business relies on a constant flow of new customers, it's critical that your team isn't nicey nice on day one and then rudely telling people, "Yeah. Take a seat over there" by the fifth visit. Whether an appointment needs to be changed or a parent is waiting near the front desk while their child is being treated, every moment of the journey must be memorable in a positive way so that your current customers tell your potential customers what a great experience they had. Positive reviews and referrals feed the initial moment of truth for the next customer.

While the clinical quality is, of course, shaped by you, the provider in a practice, your customer's first impression—and every step of their journey—is shaped by your front desk team. That's why front desk people are practice champions. They're the only ones present at every instance in the Moments of Truth journey that happens within your business.

The beauty of training to change habits is that we have proven business principles on our side. There are several that I find to be extremely useful when it comes to changing habits. If we understand these principles, it makes it easier to know how to respond in any situation.

Huddle Up

- o **Have you developed a communications plan for your front desk?**
- o **What kind of customer excellence training does your team undergo?**
- o **How consistent is the experience your practice provides?**
- o **Have you ever employed any of the principles covered in this chapter?**

Chapter 3

Business Principles

A STRONG, CONFIDENT PERSON CAN RULE THE ROOM WITH KNOWLEDGE, PERSONAL STYLE, ATTITUDE, AND GREAT POSTURE.

—CINDY ANN PETERSON

Some of the people in our lives just seem to naturally know how to communicate. Grandpa, for instance, may have a knack for knowing just what to say to get us to act. Maybe you remember sitting at the table with him when you were young and putting together a puzzle. It may have seemed like a game to you, but Grandpa knew exactly how to guide you to a better understanding of the end goal. "Come on Johnny, you can do it. Try that puzzle piece. Turn it around. You need some help? Oh, look, you've got it. Let's do the next piece." All along, he's challenging and pushing you forward yet also gently asking, "Where do you need help? How can I help you?"

What Grandpa was doing was moving seamlessly between what are known as "postures." Although posture is typically thought of as sitting tall or standing up straight, it also relates to different frames of mind or attitudes when communicating with our customers.

Postures are one of the business principles that can help your team communicate. While people such as Grandpa may just naturally understand the principles of communication, most of us want and need to know why and how these principles work.

To better understand them, let's first look at a very foundational principle of communication.

Cialdini's Six Principles

One of the communications concepts that I've adapted to my coaching comes from Dr. Robert Cialdini's Six Principles of Persuasion, which he presents in his book *Influence*. He formed these concepts after he studied some of the practices that salespeople use during their pitches.

Studies have found that these principles actually work. For instance, one experiment found that simply leaving a mint when the tab for a meal is placed on the table can increase tips by 3 percent.[2]

Here is some explanation of the principles and some of the ways we can apply them.

Liking. People are influenced by others they like. So how do we help people like us? We need to provide opportunities for them to be drawn to us. That means making sure your website posts your biography, that your office has personal touches that speak to more than just your medical training. If you like cats, let people know it. If you like sailing, let people know. Those personal touch points let people find commonalities that can help them open up to you.

Reciprocity. This is about repaying kindness. It's why we're polite to others: so that they can feel comfortable being polite to us. It's also why we feel indebted to others. When someone gives us a gift at Christmas, we feel indebted to give one back. If someone is kind

---

2   "Principles of Persuasion," Influence at Work, accessed June 22, 2019, https://www.influenceatwork.com/principles-of-persuasion/.

to us, we tend to reflect that kindness back to them.

Authority. Authority works because we tend to submit to or be influenced by people in authority or who are perceived to be in authority. I sometimes call this the "white coat syndrome." If the doctor says so, then it's so. It's why commercials say, "Three out of four dentists say ..." It is why we use the doctor's name in some of our scripting because their authority commands attention.

Social proof. We want to do what others do. As much as we say we want to be individuals, we want to make sure that if Suzy Q., an influencer, is doing something, then we're doing it too. It's why we say, "Oh, we have other patients from that school as well," or, "Oh yes, we are very successful at getting arrangements for many families."

Scarcity. When there's less of something, we've got to have more of it. So if we say something like "I happen to have an appointment open tomorrow," then we're making that appointment all the more important.

Consistency. When people promise to do something, they tend to follow through with it. It's why instead of giving a patient a suggestion by saying, "Let us know if you need to change this appointment," we ask for a small promise: "If you need to change this appointment, will you give me a call so we can reserve the time for someone else?" When they agree to do so, "Oh, yes, I will," they are on the hook with themselves to follow through with their small promise to call you if they cannot make their appointment.

The "Know-Like-Trust" Principle

Hand-in-hand with Cialdini's principles is what I like to call the "Know-Like-Trust" Principle. If people know you, like you, and trust you, they're more likely to say yes to you. That, after all, is our ultimate goal.

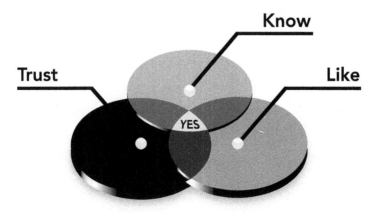

Fig. 3.1. The "Know-Like-Trust" Principle

People get to know us through the details about us on our websites, through reviews and referrals, and elsewhere. As they start connecting with us, that spills over into liking us. I have never met Oprah Winfrey or Ellen DeGeneres or Matt McConaughey, and yet I can say I like or even *love* them because I know so much about them. That's an easy spillover.

Trust, however, is a little harder to build. How do we build trust? Author Brené Brown, in *Rising Strong*, tells how she asked her daughter, "How do you know who to trust?" Some of the examples her daughter gave were "Well, she's the one who smiled when I smiled at her," "She's the one that said 'Hi' when I said 'Hi,'" and, "She's the one that sat next to me at school." It's the little things that build trust. Like filling a jar with marbles, one marble for every little bit of kindness you experience. As the jar fills, you realize you're beginning to feel trust.

Someone who upholds trust is authentic—and consistent. It means to be who you are. While you will adapt to others, you do not pretend to be someone you are not. Lack of trust is why consumers sometimes don't want to pay for services up front. They think they'll be treated differently once there is no longer a balance due. And that's not the way to build trust. We have to be consistent through the entire journey.

> Lack of trust is why consumers sometimes don't want to pay for services up front.

Along with Cialdini's Principles and Know-Like-Trust, there are two primary postures that we use throughout the day to help us improve the customer experience: deference and guidance.

Deference and Guidance Postures

Merriam-Webster's Dictionary says that deference is "respect and esteem due a superior or an elder" and that it "implies a yielding or submitting to another's judgment or preference out of respect or reverence."

Simply put, deference is about being polite and courteous—an appropriate posture for anyone working at the front desk. Examples of when this is used include when we

- offer a greeting such as "How may I help you?";

- ask someone their permission to place them on hold: "May I place you on a brief hold?";

- wrap up a conversation by asking, "Is there anything else I can do for you?"

Deference includes leaving space to be able to help once the question is asked. That occurs at the beginning and end of a call and anytime in between. For instance, we leave space to actually help after the greeting, "How may I help you?" At the end of the call, it's leaving space after asking, "Is there anything else I can do for you?" Just ending a call with "If there's anything else, let us know" and then hanging up isn't leaving space. Subtle differences like leaving space show that we're thinking of the other person. What's the interaction like from their perspective?

The other posture, guidance, is about providing direction, leadership, and advice. Instead of asking "What do you want?" it's being the wise sage in charge of a situation who says, "Let's get you scheduled. We need to do this next step." It's leading as a guide.

Guiding, politely guiding, is appropriate even in an elective-based business. Examples of guidance include when we're

- setting appointments and say, "The doctor can see you at [Option A] or [Option B]. Which one works best for you?";

- advising about the best option with "My recommendation is to ...";

- providing awareness of consequences by saying, "Yes, we can look for a late appointment, but that will impact treatment time. Do you wish for me to continue to look for the last appointment of the day or explore an option closer to what the doctor recommended?"

Guiding is important when setting up appointments in order to keep the office flow in check. If we were to give everyone the appointment they wanted, we'd be sitting around most of the day and then be super busy at five o'clock. Guiding also helps ensure procedures are scheduled appropriately based on their complexity. It's not up to the patient to tell us when they want to come in; we have to guide them to the best fit in the schedule and ensure we all share the available appointments.

The Front Office—Your Leaders

It's critical that the members of the front office team understand these postures and use them throughout the day. As the people who are setting the impression for your office, your front desk personnel are your leaders.

Sometimes, we think of the front desk as the lowliest person in our office. They're not clinicians. They're not the doctor. They're not the manager. They're not the patient coordinator. But they have more power and influence that we realize. Being a leader is more than simply a title.

CBS News told a story about Curtis, a school bus driver in Dallas, Texas, who is a great example of what I mean.[3] We tend to label school bus drivers as simply ... school bus drivers. But Curtis is so much more. He treats the students on his bus like they are professionals. He makes them responsible for the bus ride being a good experience. He shows his caring and kindness through other acts such as giving the children gifts selected for each of them. Some of the gifts fulfill a want or need; some are intended to inspire the child to keep pursuing an area in which they excel. So why is Curtis a leader? Because he has taken charge of his role. He has recognized that he is more than a bus driver; he is a positive influence on young people. He made a job that is often labeled as less important into a role that is vitally important in the lives of others.

Your strongest leaders are those team members who know how to toggle seamlessly between the postures of deference and guidance. While everyone on the team must understand and use

---

3   Steve Hartman, "'He's the Father That I Always 'Wanted': Texas School Bus Driver Gives More Than Just a Ride," CBS News, May 24, 2019, accessed June 25, 2019, https://www.cbsnews.com/news/curtis-jenkins-lake-highlands-elementary-bus-driver-beloved-by-community-2019-05-24/.

the proper posture at the proper time, no one needs it more than the people at the front desk and those who answer your phones. Why? Even without visible cues of body language, callers can perceive posture and attitude over the phone—whether someone is smiling while they talk or just trying to get you off the phone so they can get back to their lunch.

The Dance of Conversation

He who asks the questions is in control, right? Not necessarily. Just because someone is asking questions doesn't mean they are guiding the conversation. It comes down to the types of questions asked and the posture being employed.

Too often, our front desk people have a mantra in their heads: "The customer's always right." That leads to a mousy, almost cowering kind of mindset, one where they're ready to give the customer whatever they want to keep them from getting upset or from posting a bad review online. But even in the mode of deference we can still be powerful—politeness doesn't have to be mousy.

> But even in the mode of deference we can still be powerful—politeness doesn't have to be mousy.

Our front desk team must guide customers to what is needed and to what is possible. To do that, we've got to master deference and guidance in the way we ask questions. Moving back and forth between deference and guidance is a little like a dance in which the front desk leads, guiding the customer through their journey.

There are several types of questions used in that dance of conversation.

Deferring. Deferring questions are polite questions that uncover information. "Are there any other questions?" These questions typically start a conversation: "How may I help you?" Deferring questions are often followed up with guiding questions.

Clarifying. This is a type of guiding question. A clarifying question is looking for validation. "What I thought I heard you say was 'this and this and this.' Is that correct?" Someone who asks a clarifying question is still in control of the conversation.

Discovery. This is the type of question we use most often on a new inquiry call. The challenge is to use more open-ended questions rather than only close-ended questions in order to elicit coversation instead of data-gathering.

Leading. This is another type of guiding question. A leading question passes over a limited amount of control by providing limited options: "I have this and this available. Which would you prefer?"

Wishing. These are the kinds of questions we don't want to use. Wishing questions can make it sound like there are many options available. "Do either of those work?" is a type of wishing question because it doesn't lead; instead, it makes it sound like there are a lot of options. "Would you like to come in then?" and "Okay?" are more wishful questions that tend to get asked at the front desk.

All too often, team members are unaware that they're guilty of what I call the switcheroo. A classic example of the switcheroo is when a receptionist *tells* a caller they will be put on hold. "I'm going to put you on hold," they'll say. But then they return with a broadly *asked* question about setting up an appointment. "So when do you want to come in?" That's wishy washy and inconsistent and implies you have twenty-four seven availability.

It's backward. It needs to be reversed. Instead of *telling* the caller that they are going to be put on hold, we *ask* for their permission:

"May I place you on a brief hold while I do this?" Then we guide them in their options: "We have this or this available. Which one works best for you?"

Wishing questions will only make you wish you had a better trained team. But once your team understands the principles I've mentioned and masters how to employ them in your practice, your customers, patients, and potential patients—and you—will see a noticeable difference.

We'll use posture principles throughout the road map that I'm going to explain in part two of this book. But first, let's look at one more foundational piece—the personality guide.

Huddle Up

- o Have you listened to phone calls to see if your team members understand the principles of deference and guidance?
- o As a manager, have you paid attention to the questions and statements that your front desk team is asking?
- o Have you heard how your team answers the phone? Are they *telling* people they're putting them on hold, or are they *asking* for their permission to be put on hold?

Chapter 4

A Guide to Personality

HOW WE CONNECT AND PERSUADE IS AFFECTED BY THE WAY WE CHOOSE TO DELIVER THE MESSAGE.

—BERNADETTE JIWA

My oldest son, Jesse, has a very strong personality. His personality is so distinct that at one of his pediatric visits when he was around two, his pediatrician—who only saw him for minutes at a time—turned to me and said, "Amy, you're going to have your hands full. Jesse is wired to play tug-of-war, and he's going to play tug-of-war his entire life. Your challenge is not to get him to stop playing tug-of-war but to get him playing on your team instead of against you."

Those words have held true. Now in his late twenties, Jesse has been playing tug-of-war his entire life. He's wired to debate; he loves it. He challenges the status quo and is a thought leader.

I, on the other hand, am wired for order and predictability. When communicating with Jesse, what I've had to learn—and remember—is that it's not my job to get him to behave like me, or for me to behave like him, but for us to make a connection. When Jesse was sixteen, he would get frustrated, and I would almost want to shy away from the debate. Then one day he told me, "But Mom,

I love debating with you; it's who I am." That has helped me to remember that I'm not there to change him. I'm there to meet him where he is. I realize that it may feel a little uncomfortable to me, but it helps us connect, and then I can go be myself.

> Sometimes we have to come out of our natural behaviors in order to meet the other person where they are, in order to make the communication or the connection.

Sometimes we have to come out of our natural behaviors in order to meet the other person where they are, in order to make the communication or the connection.

A great illustration by Laurie Beth Jones, who wrote *The Four Elements of Success*, is about a fighter jet refueling in midair—the task can't be done without an aircraft that naturally behaves differently during flight. During refueling, the fighter jet has to slow down, which doesn't feel natural, and the fuel tanker has to speed up, which doesn't feel natural. But those acts are necessary in order to make the connection and complete the task of transferring the fuel. Once that transfer is complete, they can both go back to their natural behaviors.

As we move forward and build call sheets in the next section, we'll look at the four elements as personality guides. Each element needs something, and that's what is built into the new patient call sheet and into our training scenarios. Understanding the personalities can help us adapt based on who we are talking with; we can adapt our scripting while still sticking with a format and structure even though everyone is different.

Know Your Personalities

Whether in college or as part of job training at some point in time, as the owner of your business, you've likely been exposed to some sort of personality assessment. But often, those team members at your front desk have not had the benefit of participating in one. For them, a personality assessment is a gift that can help them grow and become more comfortable in their roles.

Most personality assessments are based on a four-quadrant classification. Whether it's DiSC (dominance, influence, steadiness, and conscientiousness) or Myers–Briggs or another personality assessment system, we all typically fall into one of four types of personalities. I like to use the Path Elements system created by Laurie Beth Jones because it employs four physical elements to identify the four classifications of personalities. I find that of all the assessments available, the four elements make it easier for people to remember their own personality, which helps them better understand other people's personalities. I gave the Path Elements assessment to my kids when they were in middle school. We all still remember our results, and they have helped us communicate with each other over the years.

Here are some of the traits of Jones's four elements. At their core, these elements somewhat align with other assessments. For instance, if you're familiar with the DiSC assessment, fire equates to D, wind equates to i, water to S, and earth to C.

- **Fire.** Fires are expressive and dominant yet need options and authority. Fires help ignite things and get things going. Fires sometimes need to quiet their opinion because somebody else might have a good idea as well. We need to give fires options and authority by making sure that we offer appointments in a way that really resonates with them.

- **Wind.** Winds are communicative; they're pollinators. They tend to be impulsive rather than logical. But sometimes winds are a little too communicative—they need to let others get a word in edgewise. Winds want flexibility and attention. We're going to give them some open-ended questions that allow them to really fully express themselves.

- **Water.** Waters are sensitive and emotional. They are the great lovers of the world. But, at times, waters need to toughen up. They feel they need to conduct an opinion poll from the entire world before making a decision. Waters need direction and kindness. We need to be sure to ask them questions like "Is there anything else I can do to help you?" to help them feel loved and then guide them by telling them how to take the next step.

- **Earth.** Earths are practical, detailed, and sometimes perfectionists. These are the people who ground chaos and provide order. As an earth myself, I sometimes find that I need to chill out or loosen up. Earths need details and the time to think about their decisions.

While the elements are great for team building, my goal with the assessment is to enable us to understand why our callers, patients, potential patients, and responsible parties respond the way they do. The key is to understand the most dominant of the personalities that we're dealing with so that we can more quickly build an experience with a new customer or potential patient.

How does understanding these personalities help in different scenarios? Let's use an example of a first-time call from a new patient. The first call that comes into the practice is traditionally handled in a very earthy way. The team member traditionally handles the call using an intake form that is basically a bullet list. *What's your name? What's your date of birth? What's your address? What's your child's name? What's their date of birth? What's your insurance?* That first call is usually very data driven, very fact finding. If you understand the traits of a wind or water personality and that's the person on the other end of the call, then it becomes obvious why they feel like they're just a number.

Leveraging the Personalities

There is much that we can glean from the four personalities and use as we design and orchestrate new patient calls and other conversations. That's how to get the best leverage.

Take, for instance, fire and earth personalities. These two personalities tend to be just-the-facts kind of people. Think, in general, of attorneys (fire) and accountants or engineers (earth). They don't want a dog and pony show; they just want the bottom line. So whether on the phone or in the office for an exam, it's important to get to the point for these two personalities. Calls and exams with either of these personalities tend to be shorter.

Whereas with water or wind personalities, launching right into the facts is a real turnoff. Again, generalizing, but waters are people more along the lines of a yoga instructor, while winds are theatrical people or salesmen. They would rather start an interaction with a little chitchat, a little conversation about their lovely shoes or what a great weekend they had. They'd rather sit and visit than know the details of an exam. These personalities need to be allowed a minute to express themselves. Starting with the facts for either of these personalities could make them immediately feel like they're just a number or just another sale. Not surprisingly, compared to fire or earth people, calls and exams with these personalities tend to take longer.

Understanding the personality you're dealing with can also improve your same-day sign-up numbers. With fire and wind, for instance, it's important to strike while the iron is hot. Both of these personalities are typically ready to get started *now*—but for different reasons. Fires want to get started now because it means they will finish sooner, whereas winds are ready to go because they are more impulsive. You might hear them say, "What a great idea. Sounds like fun. Let's do it!"

Earths and waters, on the other hand, often need to go home and think about it. Pushing either one of these personalities for a same-day commitment is more likely to upset them because they really do *need to go home and think about it.* Either of them might be up for a small commitment on the same day but not a full commitment. And they have different reasons for delaying a decision. Earths have to process the idea very slowly. They need to go home and make a spreadsheet, plot out every month of payment, and compare those to their monthly budget to make sure the plan fits. Waters, meanwhile, need to take an opinion poll. They've got to ask their friends "Will you still like me if I do this? What do you think? What should I do?"

> Because everyone is different,
> every call will be different. Instead of rigidly sticking to a structure and format, we need to be able to read the person and then adapt to what their personality needs.

The key is to be willing to adapt and to have the autonomy to do so. Because everyone is different, every call will be different. Instead of rigidly sticking to a structure and format, we need to be able to read the person and then adapt to what their personality needs. That's why a book of scripts on its own doesn't work. You've got to read your caller, read the person you are interacting with, and then meet them in the middle.

It's also what makes our front desk jobs so very interesting—it can't be done by robots.

It's why we need astute people at the front desk. When a person has the skills but not the right character, no real emotional IQ, they're more likely to follow the script without being able to adapt.

Just Imagine ...

Understanding the different personalities also means recognizing that everyone who is different from you isn't just trying to frustrate you or frustrate a situation. Their personality is almost a part of their DNA.

In my experience as a coach, the personality assessment is one of the most enlightening and enjoyable parts of training. Imagine the difference in your office when everyone understands and is more accepting of the different personalities. In fact, I've seen that assessment and training create better relationships between the team and doctor. Let me give you an example.

In one office, the doctor was a fire/earth type. He was a very intense, very practical personality who felt that all his team did was present him with problems. "They can't seem to fix anything and only bring me problems with no solutions," he said.

From the team's perspective, however, he was just scary. One team member shared with me how he always seemed frustrated and that she had been trying for a year to get him to decide on a thank-you gift for patients when they finished treatment.

After the training, the team member realized that she needed to appeal to his traits of needing options and authority. So she made a bulleted list of three gifts, and under each item, she noted the unit cost, the color, manufacture time, and shipping time. She handed the paper to the doctor, and within a day she had his decision. She had finally communicated with him in a way that met his point of need.

Interestingly, afterward, the doctor's appraisal of his team reversed. "My team is really smart," he told me.

Simply knowing how to meet the other person who's different from you is so empowering.

Now that we've laid the foundation and you have a better understanding of why we do things, let's look at some ways to put your knowledge to practical use—with how we work the plan.

Huddle Up

- **Have you ever been frustrated by different personalities in your office and been unsure what to do with them? Are these people just different from you, or do you think they're really trying to frustrate you?**

Consider giving your team the gift of the Path Elements personality assessment. Go to lauriebethjones.com.

A great use of your time and training investment is a team-building exercise around personalities.

Provide the gift of a personality assessment to your teen. You'll find great value in being able to communicate and connect with each other.

Part II

It's Your Call: The Road Map

Thus far, we've talked about how patients willing to self-pay for treatment are looking for more than quality care; they are looking for an experience. We've learned that plans work if you work the plan. We've laid the posture principles on the table, and we've dissected all you need to know about personality navigation.

Now it's time to work the plan because it's really all about execution. We'll look at how making small repeatable habits can enhance the experience.

In this section, I am sharing tips about the front desk presence on the phone and in person. Included in these chapters are instructions, scenarios, and essentially, the road map for creating an exceptional journey for patients and potential patients and customers. As you'll find in reading through these chapters, I'll refer back to the business principles and other elements that I discussed in previous chapters as these are, again, the foundational components on which you will build a team that communicates excellence.

Chapter 5

First and Last Responses— and More

POLITENESS IS TO HUMAN NATURE WHAT WARMTH IS TO WAX.

—ARTHUR SCHOPENHAUER

My young nephew has a type of disability called prune belly syndrome. It's a problem that has his parents—my sister and her husband—in and out of doctors' offices all the time. Doctors basically rule their lives.

When my brother-in-law heard about the coaching and training I provide for people working the front desk, he was amazed. "I don't think I've ever heard someone from a doctor's office starting off a call with us by being polite," he said. "I would be blown away if anyone ever treated us that way."

It's surprising how often we think that the front desk automatically knows how to handle a call with a patient or potential patient or customer. But too often, that's just not true. Would you want to go anywhere

> Would you want to go anywhere for service if the staff treated you with anything but politeness and understanding?

for service if the staff treated you with anything but politeness and understanding? Think of the difference it would make to my sister and her husband if they were greeted by a polite, friendly voice while dealing with their son's chronic illness.

Politeness from the front desk isn't unique to the medical world. Think about the last time you had an issue with your computer. Was the technician on the other end of the line courteous and helpful? Did he or she make you feel hope that there might actually be a resolution to your problem? Or were you just treated like a number in a queue and ultimately made to feel like they couldn't care less about you or your problem?

Now, I get it; the people at the front desk are busy. They may be doing any or all of the following tasks: scheduling appointments, taking money, verifying insurance, scanning documents, mailing correspondence, and answering phone calls—to name a few. Still, regardless of the task, as I've mentioned, their *role* is to be an ambassador, to welcome patients, represent the practice, and to create an amazing environment for patients and customers so that they can have a memorable journey. The goal of my coaching and training is to help front desk staff better understand that more global mindset. It's like the story about the man that passed a construction site and asked three different bricklayers what they were doing. The first looked down at his work and gruffly said, "I'm laying bricks."

The second looked up at his work and said, "I'm building a wall."

The third looked skyward in awe and said, "I am building a cathedral!"

More than just telling your team what to do, part of my learning platform is to help those whom I'm coaching understand *why* we're doing what we're doing. When we're toddlers, asking "Why? Why?" is the norm. But by the time we're adults, we're often trained to just do and not ask why. We're told to just "do it better" or we're told to "memorize this," but we're not given any understanding of what that means or why it's important. I don't want the crucial staff members to simply be robots. If they can connect the dots between the training and their jobs, then the habits they're learning will stick better.

As part of the training, I give them how-to examples, ask them to demonstrate the training they've been shown, and then provide feedback. Simply having the knowledge doesn't mean we know how to do something; often, what we're doing is a lot different from what we think we're doing. That's why feedback from a coach is so important. Commonly, feedback comes from mystery calls who are designed to play "gotcha" with a team member and slam them for "doing it wrong." I want team members to be able to go about their normal day but to develop new habits that they can use on every call and with every interaction. My tools include recordings of calls that I can play back for the trainee to hear and better understand the subtle differences in what's being said and how that impacts your patients and potential patients and customers. My goal as a coach is not to play "gotcha"; it's to empower them to perform by providing repeatable actions to help build habits.

> Simply having the knowledge doesn't mean we know how to do something; often, what we're doing is a lot different from what we think we're doing.

In this part of the book, I'm sharing some basic lessons to address common issues. Each can be tailored to your team. The first of these lessons is about first and last responses, basically how we open and close a conversation. With both of these, we use the posture of deference or politeness.

Saying Hello—Opening the Conversation

The first response occurs when answering the phone from a caller. We give the greeting, "Thank you for calling Communicate Excellence. This is Amy. How may I help you?"

The caller then tells us why they're calling, whatever the reason: "I'm calling to reschedule," "I'm calling to find out what time my appointment is." The very next thing we say is our first response.

Imagine when you call a doctor's office—what is usually the first response? "What's your name?" or "What's your date of birth?" And it comes across in an almost nasally tone. In fact, we've become so attuned to flat first responses when we call up an office that we start giving our name and date of birth in our first comments.

First responses are often included in scripts for new patient calls, but they can come across as cheesy: "Fantastic. You have just called the right place." Sounding cheesy is worse than if the response is missing altogether. A first response must be authentic.

The first response we give to a customer is an opportunity to create an impression and make the most of a moment of truth. And whether it's a new patient—someone who's never interacted with your office—or an existing patient, the first response helps form or maintain the impression of your office. It is a pleasantry before business. In this day and age, where common courtesy has become uncommon, the first response is a real opportunity to surprise the caller. As authors Chip and Dan Heath explain in their book *The Power of Moments: Why Certain Experiences Have*

> In this day and age, where common courtesy has become uncommon, the first response is a real opportunity to surprise the caller.

Extraordinary Impact, if you can surprise someone, it can basically shake them out of the numbness that we tend to develop as we go about our busy days. That helps lock in that moment of truth. It's the same kind of reaction that my brother-in-law had when I told him about the coaching.

First responses are simply a matter of authentically saying, "I would be happy to help you."

First responses work because we drop in an emotion word. "I would be *happy* to help you. I would be *glad* to help you." That's all we're doing. And while the person on the other end of the line is probably not going to say, "Whoa, I've never heard that," you can almost sense their positive reaction. Even though we can't see a smile, we can hear their smile, and we convey ours.

Don't simply use your tone to express your happiness to help them. Say it with words.

Saying Goodbye—Closing the Conversation

Last responses are a little easier to grasp than first responses. Last responses happen on the back end of a call, and many times our team members are already using them.

However, just like first responses, last responses need to be authentic—and intentional. As we begin to wrap up the call, instead of just having the conversation fall off and end with a "bye-bye," we want to be sure to insert another pleasantry—in fact, we want there to be pleasantry before business, just like on the front end of the call. Instead of just saying, "See you Monday at ten o'clock. Bye-bye," we say, "See you Monday at ten o'clock. Have a good weekend." That's how to leave a last impression.

First and last responses wrap the conversation in an envelope of politeness. Imagine someone has gone to a store and bought you a gift for your birthday. They didn't have time to wrap it, and they handed it to you in the store's bag. Compare that to someone who bought you the gift, took it home, took time to wrap it, put a bow on it to embellish it, and then gave it to you. It's the same gift, but there's something about the presentation of it that stands apart. Presentation is everything.

The same concept changes the tone for our calls. We're taking the exact same conversation and enveloping it in a great presentation. It surprises patients, potential patients, and potential customers while also subtly teaching them how to treat us. Now, suddenly, they realize, "Hey, this is a place that does politeness."

How to Hold

Another posture of deference, or politeness, is how we handle putting people on hold. I've discussed this from the perspective of wishing and guiding. Here, I want to reiterate that we are asking permission but also *setting expectations*. Instead of "I'm placing you on hold," we use, "May I place you on a brief hold while I …?" The "while I" creates a visual picture for the caller: "while I check the calendar," "while I ask the doctor," or, "while I look up the schedule." Whatever the case may be, we ask for permission and then create a visual to help set expectations.

Compare this to getting on a plane with an airline pilot who doesn't communicate. We get on the plane, they quickly shut the door, they roll us back out to the tarmac, and there we sit, growing more and more frustrated. But if the pilot gets on the intercom and announces, "Ladies and gentlemen, I apologize for the delay. Traffic control has told us that we will have wheels up in ten minutes. If there are any other updates, I will let you know." Well, you look at your watch and you say, "Okay." You're not thrilled about it, but at least you've had your expectations set. Without updates, you're a lot more frantic and a lot more frustrated.

When we put someone on hold and we give them a reason, it helps them better understand what to expect. There's a subtle but important difference between "May I place you on a brief hold while I do this?" and what I commonly hear, which is "Do you mind holding?" or even "I'm going to place you on hold." Asking "May I," as I've mentioned, requests their permission, whereas "Do you mind" implies that you're going to put them on hold anyway.

There are subtle differences when picking up after a hold as well. I refer to these as the three Ps, standing for politeness, practicality, and pause:

- **Politeness in general.** This is simple; they waited for us, so we thank them. Starting off with "Thank you for holding" sets the right tone and pace.

- **Practicality for them.** In the past, when phones were corded, we couldn't get too far away after being placed on hold. Today, cell phones let us walk around and work and do things while we're waiting. Or in many instances, the person will place the cell phone on speaker and then start doing something else. So thanking them for holding gives them enough time to realize "They're back." They can stop checking Facebook, stop unloading the dishwasher, whatever they were doing. It gives them a moment to switch gears—to take the phone off speaker and get ready to hear you.

- **Pause and breathe for us.** Instead of slamming right into the conversation, we must take a breath and watch how fast we speak. If you're like me and you've been scrambling around trying to find an answer and you're hurrying back to the phone, you may get in such a hurry that you slam right into it. "Oh my goodness, okay, I've got an answer for you. Blah, blah, blah." Instead, take a breath before speaking.

It's during the first and last responses, and when handling calls that get placed on hold, that our teams tend to get the postures of deference and guidance backward. (Remember the switcheroo in chapter 3?) Once they understand these postures, however, we can begin to do an about-face on how they set appointments.

Huddle Up

o When was the last time you listened in on a call to see how your team members address your patients, potential patients, and potential customers?

o When you listen in on your team's calls, are you hearing what you want to hear?

o When you call an office for an appointment, to ask a question, or to get information about a service, how do they treat you? How does that make you feel?

Chapter 6

Setting Appointments

WHEN PLACED IN COMMAND—TAKE CHARGE.

—GEN. NORMAN SCHWARZKOPF JR.

Have you ever been to a McDonald's PlayPlace or any playground and seen a mom trying to get her child to go home? "Johnny, we're going to go home. Okay? Okay?" You can almost see mom scrunching up her face and hunching her shoulders. You can hear the lilt in their voice. That's a wish, not an instruction.

Contrast that to the mom who says, "Johnny, we are going in five minutes. Do you understand?"

"Yes ma'am. Yes, Mom."

Which one was more effective? It's very obvious. In the first example, Johnny's not going to comply. He's just going back to the playground. "No, Mom. No," and off he goes. In the second example, there is guidance. The question is to clarify understanding, not to pass authority to the child.

Too often, our front desk individuals are just wishing to make an appointment. They're almost pleading with the patient: "Please take one," like the mom pleading with Johnny to leave the playground. Ever wonder why you have days that are absolutely a zoo? It's because a powerless front desk person is setting appointments using wishing techniques and getting bullied into whatever the customer is insisting on. It happens when your appointment setters are letting your patients take charge, and you end up with everyone coming in after school or at the end of the workday.

In contrast, I want your front desk people to see themselves as guides. If you were climbing one of the world's tallest peaks, you would hire a guide to help get you there. You would want someone who knows what to expect—the reality of the cold and wind and lack of oxygen. You would want someone who knows and can explain everything that will happen. It is the guide's job to give us options and authority. If I get tired and, thinking in a shortsighted manner, ask to rest, it is up to a good guide to say: "Amy, we could stop and rest, but if we do, we're not getting to the summit today. And if we don't reach the summit today, the season will close, and it will be next year before we can try again. Which do you want—do you want to make it to the summit, or do you want to delay until next year?" Such a response helps me see whether I would rather have my short-term desire met or my ultimate goal of reaching the summit obtained.

While the wishing and pleading team member is weak and mousy, the guide is powerful and confident without being bossy or mean. The guide is simply providing information and then helping your callers to a solution.

Immediate versus Ultimate Goal

A guide is someone who knows how to remind callers of the long-term goal—something that's easy to lose sight of when it comes to treatment. The short-term goal is making the appointment today. For the caller—your patient or potential patient—that means getting an appointment that seems the most convenient. But four weeks from today, that appointment may not be convenient anymore, and then they're going to try to reschedule and push that appointment out. A guide can help them remember that they're trading short-term inconvenience today for the long-term win tomorrow.

Setting appointments uses the posture of guidance to help patients understand the difference between immediate and ultimate goals. The immediate goal is an easy appointment. An ultimate goal is getting done with treatment. Compare that to someone wanting to lose weight. They're not looking forward to all that it's going to take to shed pounds, but they are looking forward to feeling better about themselves and fitting into smaller clothes.

> The immediate goal is an easy appointment. An ultimate goal is getting done with treatment.

From the standpoint of a patient who is undergoing treatment with braces, the ultimate goal is to have a good smile. They're not looking forward to the treatment itself or to having to be monitored for months on end until that treatment is complete; they are looking forward to having the braces removed or the treatment coming to an end—and having a whole new smile. The same goes for someone wanting to have their body reshaped. They're not looking forward to the treatment itself or to managing their treatment postprocedure. But they are definitely looking forward to having a new figure or face posttreatment. What actually drives them to you and your practice is their ultimate goal— to have a new smile, a new body.

However, in the process of helping people reach their goals, we're asking them to use up their time, and that's something they forget. In that moment when they're on the phone with your team, thinking about scheduling their calendar, they're only thinking about the immediate: "Let's wait until baseball season is over," or, "Let's see when you have an opening at four thirty in the afternoon." They momentarily forget their ultimate goal.

Yes, we can help them. We can most certainly find a time in the schedule based on "the customer is always right." But it's up to our team to let them know the consequences: "Mrs. Jones, I can certainly look for that late appointment, but it will mean waiting another month, which adds that month on to the time in treatment." We have to help them come to their senses, to help them remember what they ultimately want.

By being powerful in their roles, your front desk team is not only helping patients reach their goals but also fulfilling their role of managing your schedule based on your capacity. As I've mentioned, we can't possibly accommodate 90 percent of the appointments that we see in a day between four thirty and six o'clock, or 25 percent of our hours. That's not good for business, and in reality, it's not possible—it's simply not possible to give everyone what they want in the way of scheduling.

Keeping everyone happy and keeping the schedule filled comes down to how we offer the appointments. It's not about being mean or harsh; it's simply being a guide.

Best Practices for Scheduling

When scheduling appointments, our front desk team members are the predictors of the success or nonsuccess of the future. They are our fortune tellers. There are grids that we need to fill with patients, and those grids predict how the practice operates for the next six, eight, twelve weeks or more. How those days are scheduled sets the practice up for success—or not. Schedulers control the flow because they cannot cheat the amount of time committed to the doctor or doctors. There are fewer doctors in a practice than there are people and staff in the clinic.

Think of an air traffic controller. Do you ever think they are negotiating with a pilot? A pilot would not dare say, "Yeah, that looks like there's a big enough gap. I'm going to squeeze in there." Nope, the air traffic controller isn't having any of that. Front desk schedulers should not allow that either—they should not allow patients just to slip in whenever, wherever they want. When scheduling patients for treatment, the scheduler must understand not only how each day runs and its timing but also whether there is enough time for quality care without rushing.

When it comes to scheduling, our front desk team must remember that they command the schedule and are there to help the customer *and* the practice. They must remember their role as a guide.

Here are some best practices that schedulers should use to keep the practice humming.

Give Limited Options

Even though not everyone being scheduled is a fire personality, the scenario itself is. We all want to control our own calendars—that's what makes it a fire scenario.

And what do fires need? Options and authority.

Options should be provided as a statement. They're facts. Options should not be offered like wishes: "I have a two o'clock. Could you come in at that time?" No. The options should be stated first, then followed by the question. "Mrs. Jones, Dr. Smile has availability at this time or this time. Which one works best for you?"

It's very hard to regain control of this scenario if it's given up by using wishing instead of options and authority. Especially when on the phone, we want to avoid having a lilt in our voice when giving options, as it makes the exchange sound more like a wish. Moreover, we must also use a follow-up question. While that follow-up question momentarily passes the authority, it helps the other person know that it is their turn to talk, and it actually keeps us from accidentally slipping the lilt into our voice when we're saying the times. Instead of, "How about eight or ten?" we want to stay in statement mode:

- Fact/options: "The doctor has these times."

- Question: "Which works best for you?"

This kind of phrasing keeps the situation from sounding like the caller is the one who's setting the appointment, and it places the lilt on the question instead of on the options.

When stating the options, the doctor's name is used as a position of authority: "Dr. Smile has this availability," or, "Dr. Smile is recommending this." This is a Cialdini principle of persuasion at work, where we are influenced by those in authority. In this case we draw on the authority a doctor's role naturally holds.

Additionally, we take care in how we phrase the question. We want to lead and guide the customer to a desired solution. That way, the caller is guided to the choices—A or B. Then that simple phrase, "Which one?" makes it sound like the choices are limited. In contrast, phrasing the options as "Do either of those work for you?" makes it sound like A and B might only be two options out of a slew of many. Limiting the choices helps keep us from getting into the time-consuming negotiation of finding two more that the caller might like, then two more, then more. By guiding them to A or B, there is a better chance they will choose one. Now, they may choose C, "none of the above," at which point we then have to find more options, but again, only two—"This or this, which one works for you?"

Even if the schedule is wide open, narrow the choices to two—early and late: "I have options as early as eight, and as late as four, with some in between. Which works best for you?" Don't confuse a caller by listing a plethora of options with crazy combinations: 8:10 a.m., 9:00 a.m. to 10:00 a.m., 11:05 a.m., 11:25 a.m., and so on. It seems easy to you because you see the list, but your customer has to visualize each of the options being offered, and that can take some hard work. Don't make them work so hard, and don't make it hard on yourself. So again, keep the options at two and the scheduling will move along far more efficiently.

> Don't make them work so hard, and don't make it hard on yourself.

Space and Silence

Once options have been provided, we hush. We sit in silence and give space for them to respond.

I remember a young woman in one office, a very sweet person with a Pollyanna-type disposition. When I first started working with her, I thought for sure she would be eaten alive by a busy mom looking to schedule an appointment for her child. As I sat there shadowing her, she said, "Mrs. Jones, I see Dr. Smile had recommended a time for you in six weeks. Dr. Smile has a one o'clock or a two o'clock. Which one works better for you?" Then she just sat there and smiled prettily. The mom was flipping through her cell phone calendar so long that even I started to get anxious—it was all I could do to avoid pointing out two other slots on the schedule that were in the "ideal" after-school hours. But I held out—and so did my Pollyanna-dispositioned coordinator. Finally, the mom said, "All right, I'll take two o'clock." I was amazed, and as I continued to shadow the young woman, she did same thing over and over again. It really worked!

Afterward, I asked the young woman about her method. "You had times later in the afternoon, yet you offered the first in the afternoons," I said. "What's your thought process?"

She answered, "Well, you told me to take control of my calendar, so I did. I start with the harder-to-schedule slots. If they take it, great. If they don't, I look like I did a wonderful thing for them by slipping down to the next hour or two. I look like a hero."

Think of it this way. Have you ever gone to a party and found yourself standing around in a circle? We do that to keep a certain amount of personal space between us and the other partygoers. Even as the group gets bigger, there's a certain amount of personal space that tends to move with us around the room. Well, the same thing happens while scheduling, whether on the phone or in person. Like the partygoers, we maintain a certain amount of "personal space" at all times—when one person leans into it, the other steps back. A question from a scheduling coordinator such as "When would you like to come in?" almost invites the person to have a seat and start thumbing through the scheduling calendar themselves. A question like that gives up control; at that point, the scheduling coordinator more or less exits their seat. And once the patient or customer puts themselves in the scheduler's seat, good luck getting them out of that seat until they've had their way. That's why schedulers must maintain control of the schedule.

Set Flexible Expectations—within Limits

If there is a limitation as to why the patient needs an appointment with certain parameters—for instance, they need a longer appointment and those are only done midmorning—then we need to say so up front. We don't want to make a patient have to figure out why. If a parent is standing in front of the scheduler being told no, they can't have a two o'clock appointment this week, then they are just going to keep asking "How about next week?" And if they hear "No, I don't have anything," the cycle will repeat itself. They think if they go out far enough, they're going to get what they want when in reality there's a limitation—there are no two o'clock appointments for the procedure that needs to be done. That needs to be stated up front. We would say, "Mrs. Jones, I see Dr. Beautiful has requested a longer appointment. That procedure will be scheduled in the ten or eleven o'clock hour. In light of that, would you prefer me to look on Monday/Tuesday or Wednesday/Thursday?" However, if there is flexibility, that should also be made known. For instance, if there's a last-minute cancellation list, that information should be shared.

One way to help set expectations is to provide a handout at the onset of treatment that explains details such as the fact that some longer appointments must be scheduled during certain times of the day. I'll talk more about resources such as this near the end of chapter 8.

Be Consistent

Whatever the message, when it comes to scheduling, consistency is key. For example, if the patient's next appointment needs to be longer, then clinical and front desk team members must share the same message. Here's how that scenario might go:

- **Doctor, as they finish their work.** "I'll be seeing you in the morning next time because we're going to be doing lots of work in that appointment."

- **Clinician, while walking the patient to the front desk.** "You will be scheduling one of our morning appointments because we're doing extra work."

- **Front desk, while getting the appointment on the calendar.** "Mrs. Jones, Dr. Smile has prescribed a longer appointment that requires greater detail. As you remember, this is one of those morning appointments we discussed, which means ten o'clock. We have Monday and Tuesday available that week. Which would be best?"

By having everyone on the same page and repeating the same message, the front desk doesn't have to be the bad guy.

Advise and Notate

At times, even guiding the patient through two options at a time will still result in them choosing option C—an option that is convenient for them but inconvenient for the practice and maybe even detrimental to their treatment timing. When that happens, we have to advise them of our recommendation and the unintended consequence. So if they continue to say, "I'm only coming in at four thirty," then that must be noted in their chart, and it's up to us to say, "Yes, I'd be glad to look at that time for you, realizing that does push us out further than intended and adds to your treatment time. Do you wish for me to continue to look for four thirty or something closer to what the doctor recommended?" By leaving the choice up to them, at least they've been made aware.

By noting such conversations, it empowers the doctor and clinical team when treatment extends beyond the original estimation. The notes help the team to be able to say, "Mrs. Jones, I see the 4:30 p.m. time was very important to you. Each requested appointment got extended by a week for a total of eight times … so in light of that extra eight weeks, we are actually ahead of our estimation."

Don't Create a "No" Scenario

We don't want to open up the schedule so much that we end up having to say "No." That's why we don't ask broad questions such as "When do you want to come in?" and we don't say, "We're open Monday through Friday" when we're closed on Wednesday.

For example, let's say the scheduler tells the caller, "We have appointments Monday through Thursday. Which of those days works best for you?" Not only is that offering too many options, it's also opening the conversation up to getting a no from the caller.

- Caller: "How about next Wednesday?"

- Scheduler: "Oh, well, we're closed on Wednesdays."

- Caller: "Do you have a six o'clock spot available?"

- Scheduler: "No, we close at five o'clock."

If an option leaves the door open to receiving a no, then we don't use it.

Acting as a guide saves time when setting appointments. By taking charge, your front desk team avoids getting into a negotiation scenario. It changes the entire feel of the calls—they become more professional, more representative of your practice. Your team can take in more calls because the process has become streamlined and professional, yet still creates a positive and memorable experience for the client. And that happens with call after call after call.

In addition to the first and last response, which we covered in the last chapter, setting appointments is the most critical thing your team does. Together, these are the building blocks that lead up to the most important phone call—the new patient or inquiry call. This call is all about bringing people in because without patients or customers you don't have a practice.

Huddle Up

o **Do you know the rules for filling your schedule?**

o **When can your scheduling rules be bent or broken to meet a customer experience need or to address a customer who has had a really poor experience?**

o **Have you created a decision tree to empower your front desk to know when and how to override the schedule to appropriately fill it?**

o **Do you need to create an A-list containing those patients who are close friends of the doctor, or a list of those who would create such bad PR that it causes more trouble than you can handle? Keep the number or percentage of these very _low._**

Chapter 7

New Patients and More

YOU CAN MAKE MORE FRIENDS IN TWO
MONTHS BY BECOMING INTERESTED
IN OTHER PEOPLE THAN YOU CAN IN
TWO YEARS BY TRYING TO GET OTHER
PEOPLE INTERESTED IN YOU.

—DALE CARNEGIE

For a long time, I wanted to see the play *Hamilton* on Broadway, but for one reason or another, I never made it. Finally, it left Broadway and was scheduled to appear at a performance hall near me. I bought my ticket and went to see the show.

Now, I knew that by the time I saw the play, those actors and actresses had been through their lines hundreds, if not thousands of times. But even so, when it was my turn to see it, I did not want to be shortchanged. I did not want them to make up lines on the fly or skip a song because they were tired of doing it. I paid for the full performance, and that's what I wanted in return. Fortunately, it did not disappoint.

In similar fashion, the first call with a patient or potential patient is an important performance by your front desk team. When I explained this concept this way in one coaching session, one member of the team had a true *aha* moment. They said, "Oh my, and our patients are paying more every time they come in to see us than they ever pay to go to a stage play." That's why it doesn't matter if it's the first call on Monday morning or the last call on Friday afternoon. Every call—every performance—must uphold the standards of your office.

There are actually several components that make up the flow of a new patient call. These components provide your team with the foundational elements to gather the information needed, yet allow for the flexibility to meander wherever the call is going, if needed.

In this chapter, I'm going to share with you these components. With these components, we're trying to increase your conversion rate and lower your no-show rate because a person interested enough to call you but not interested enough to show up to see you is *thousands* of lost dollars of revenue and marketing costs thrown to the wind.

Let's start with the format used for taking down information.

Paper versus Computer—Which Is Best?

Does this scenario sound familiar? You get on a call with the help desk, and they tell you, "I'm sorry, can you wait please? My computer's going very slow." Or worse, it takes fifteen minutes to give them all your information, very detailed information, only to have them say, "Oh no, now my computer didn't save. We need to start over. What is your name?" I have actually heard this happen more times than I wish to admit in the thousands of calls I assess each year.

You can see why I propose using paper forms for the patient intake call versus having everything computerized. True, having the form computerized aids in being able to proclaim the status of being totally paperless. But is a computerized intake form really better and faster? Well, not when you consider the scenarios I just presented.

From where I sit as a coach listening to calls, there is more evidence to support having paper on hand if you're going to make the best first impression. There are a number of reasons I propose paper over using a computer for the first call. Here are just a few:

- **Technology problems.** As I mentioned, as much as we like to rely on technology, it's not flawless. Computers can lock up at the most inconvenient time, making for a less-than-stellar experience for the caller.

- **Lack of key messages.** Software usually lacks the scripts your team needs to use in gathering information, leading to incomplete or unclear communication.

- **Data-gathering limitations.** Computer-based forms usually lack the flexibility to alter the form, if needed, to include special information about the caller. They also prevent us from "going with the flow" with caller information. I never want to hear in someone's tone, "No, no, no. Don't tell me that now; that is on screen twenty, and we are on screen two."

The first call must make the best impression. By using paper forms instead of computerized ones, your team has a better tool for ensuring that the performance goes off without a hitch.

The New Patient Intake

The caller of today is not like the caller of twenty years ago or even five years ago. These days, we don't have as many stay-at-home moms, or even if they are, they're still taking Sally and Johnny to music lessons, sports lessons, after-school activities, and between-school activities. They are busy, they are bombarded by marketing, they are on the road, and they're always on a cell phone. In short, they are distracted.

The initial call format of decades ago no longer fits their needs. We have to adapt to those needs, which means we can't have a ten-, fifteen-, twenty-minute phone call with them to pull all the information we need. They are not going to have the patience to stay on the phone with us long enough to become a patient.

> They are not going to have the patience to stay on the phone with us long enough to become a patient.

In the past, the patient intake call was all about data gathering. It was all about extracting data from the patient or, in the case of orthodontics, maybe a parent. These days, there is a real art to the patient intake call. It must be more of a back-and-forth dialogue that adds value to the conversation and takes into consideration the personalities on each end of the phone. Refer to chapter 4 for a detailed review of the four personality types—fire, earth, water, and wind.

I like to equate the call to a first date of sorts. First dates are usually pretty exciting; the first call should also be a little exciting, too—definitely more pleasure than chore. It should be as much about fostering dialogue and making a connection as it is about gathering data.

Let's look at a summary version of those components that I mentioned at the beginning of the chapter.

Introduction

The call begins by setting a tone of politeness and courtesy. From the start, it should begin making the right impression about your office.

Typically, after our first response of "I would be happy to help you," we start by getting the caller's name and then say, "In the event we get disconnected, what's the best number to use to return the call?" That is an industry standard at this point. We want to get their name and phone number. If they have to run off quickly, before we're able to finish the intake, then we need a way of getting in touch with them.

Discovery

Remember, the intake call is more of a first date than an inquisition. What pieces of information are absolutely necessary, which pieces of information are nice to have, and what can actually wait?

As part of the discovery component, we want to know name, address, and those kinds of details. If you're sending something out by e-mail to the caller, we don't need to ask for their physical address on the phone. In many practices, the patient is given a clipboard on their first visit and asked to fill out a form that also includes their address, so if we aren't going to immediately mail something to them, then we don't ask for it. Streamlining the process for busy patients-to-be means that we don't need to ask for information more than once. What can be cut out of the process? Think about it. Even if all we find out in the first call is the patient's name, phone number, and appointment date, we can gather the rest of the information we need when they come in.

Streamlining the process for busy patients-to-be means that we don't need to ask for information more than once.

Close-ended questions saturate most inquiry calls. This staccato, ping-pong effect of question-answer, question-reply is why many calls sound as if we are going down a list or tabbing through computer screens. (Please *don't*!) Don't hold them hostage. They called for an appointment. Don't make them answer all your questions first before you will allow them to get an appointment: "If you are a good caller and answer *all* my questions, *then* I will let you have what you called for—an appointment." Instead, the discovery component should start with an open-ended question. These are questions that can't be answered with a one-word answer. I like to begin with "Ms. Jones, what prompted you to call us today?" That, depending on how you emphasize it, will get people talking. It's also a question that really meets those water and wind people who are relationship oriented. They tend to tell you lots of things. They may even tell you things that were never on your question-and-answer section before.

If the patient or customer is really blunt, that's fine as well. That might be a cue that they are a fire or earth person. If it seems to be a more direct type of call, then just gather enough details to schedule, but don't get into an inquisition.

By adding strategically placed, open-ended questions through-out the inquiry call, we create space to uncover valuable information. These also foster the relationship by demonstrating a greater curiosity about the new patient. Finally, it sure feels better being asked questions in a way that makes a person want to offer information rather than having it extracted.

Think about it. Would you rather answer the typical questions: "Name? Date of birth? Address? Phone number? Who referred you?" Or would you rather experience a greater free flow and exchange of information with the following inserted throughout a call: "What prompted you to give us a call today?" and "Is there anything else we can do to make your first visit more comfortable?"

Inform/Appoint and the "Solo"

This component is about informing the caller, giving enough details, and appointing them. We provide the overview of what to expect in their appointment, such as whether it's a complimentary consult and whether they are seeing a doctor. We walk through all the details, keeping in mind the needs of the personality we're dealing with.

We also want to make sure that we're advising them by using benefit statements—telling them what's in it for them. Without those benefit statements, it can begin to sound like it's all about the practice. But if the new patient is going to offer something up—their information, in this case—they want to know what they're getting in return. For instance, when asking for the client's e-mail, we explain why: "I would love to send you appointment details. May I have an e-mail that works best for you?"

The inform/appoint component is where we let them know how they can see the doctor and have everyone get their questions answered. It also includes what I call the "solo." The solo is the front desk person's scripted words—their words—in a structure that encompasses the details they share with the new patient about their visit, the invite, and the ask.

The solo is the part of the call that often gets left out. I can't tell you how many times even brief details of how long the appointment's going to be never get mentioned. Once your team member has their solo down, the goal is to present it the same way with every call, essentially a routine.

The details part of the solo routine includes three main points for an orthodontics consultation: the overview, the doctor consult, and the wrap-up with the treatment coordinator. Here are some brief examples:

- **The overview.** This explains the amount of time the appointment will take and that photos or X-rays will be taken. Mentioning these points can help uncover any anxiety the new patient may have.

- **The doctor consult.** This is a general explanation that the doctor will do an exam and provide recommendations.

- **The wrap-up with the treatment coordinator.** This will be another general statement about how the treatment coordinator will walk them through next steps. It also includes the statement: "If treatment is recommended, the treatment coordinator will talk about financial arrangements." *If* lets the new patient know that not everyone is recommended for treatment.

Once the details are shared, then it's time for the invite. There are a number of ways to seamlessly move to the invite. One is to ask whether anyone else will be coming to the appointment after letting them know they will have time with the doctor to get all their questions answered.

After that, we move into setting the appointment, which I explained in chapter 6.

Assist

After setting the appointment, we ask how they would like a reminder to be sent to them. Again, this is formed as a benefit statement instead of just taking information: "Mrs. Jones, I would love to be able to send you an appointment reminder via e-mail. What is the best e-mail to send it to?"

Next, if insurance information is needed beforehand, it can be gathered—also in the benefits format: "In order to provide you all the information at the appointment, is there any insurance that we can verify for you in advance?"

We also want to be sure to give them space to ask questions: "Mrs. Jones, is there anything else that we can do that would make Johnny's visit more comfortable?" or "Do you have any other questions for me?" Again, the phrasing is very important here. We don't want to say, "If you have any questions, make sure you give me a call," and then move on without giving space. Instead, the phrase should be "Do you have any questions?" Then move on into the closure.

Closure

In closure, we repeat the appointment details to make sure we have that final response: "We look forward to seeing you. I hope you have a great day." When we're repeating the appointment details, we ask for a small promise. (Remember Cialdini's principles in chapter 3?)

Instead of saying, "If you need to reschedule this appointment, please give me a call," which is a suggestion, we ask for a small promise: "In the event you are unable to keep this appointment, will you call me so we can release this reserved time to someone else?" Once we have their yes, we are much more likely to receive a call to reschedule or cancel, instead of them becoming a no-show with no warning.

These components help set a great first impression while making sure we are not only in the game but the leader in the game. Most new patients can call multiple places to get various opinions. If we are not the first person they're seeing, we don't want them to go to that first or second place and think, "Oh, this place is good enough." We want them to be so curious and have such a great impression of us that they say of other practices, "This place seems fine, but that one practice I went to (your practice) was even more polite. I'm going to wait until I get a consult with them also."

Again, what we're trying to do with these components and the other tips I've shared with you in this part of the book is increase your conversion rate. We do that by having more callers—who have already begun to connect with you—*actually* show up.

No-Show Rates

Being stood up is maddening. It's one thing to know you're going to have a hole in your schedule that lets you do something else productive to fill the time, but when a scheduled patient does not show up at the last minute, it is wasted time.

Sure, we feel the impact of it in that moment, and we look at our metrics afterward to get a better idea of what just happened. But how much have you drilled down into your no-show rate?

No-show rates across the medical industry range from 15 to 30 percent, and in primary care they are sometimes as high as 50 percent.[4] These percentages come from looking at the

---

4   Michael L. Davies et al., "Large-Scale No-Show Patterns and Distributions for Clinic Operational Research," *Healthcare* 4, no. 1 (March 2016): 15.

number of appointments made versus the number of clients who didn't show up—simple math. For new patients especially, no-show rates are higher.

Let's look at the impact of no-show rates. In orthodontics, the goal no-show rate is 5 percent. But if you were to isolate the no-show rates of the new patient procedures, it is likely to be double that amount. If you were to experience, for instance, a 10 percent no-show rate with new patients, multiply that by your average case. That's money you never even had the chance to make—tens to hundreds of thousands of dollars never made it into your bank account.

Now take your marketing budget of dollars spent and multiply that by 10 percent. How many tens or hundreds of thousands of dollars did you spend to make your phone ring only to result in no one showing up? You might as well put that money in a bag and leave it at the front door of your competitor. That's what's at stake here. Once a patient has started treatment, if they don't show, their treatment doesn't progress. That's a natural consequence of not showing up. Their no-show is probably caused by something happening in their life. Maybe they simply forgot. The root causes of no-shows are many, but someone who's already begun treatment is going to call and get cycled back in because they want to keep moving toward their ultimate goal.

> How many tens or hundreds of thousands of dollars did you spend to make your phone ring only to result in no one showing up? You might as well put that money in a bag and leave it at the front door of your competitor. That's what's at stake here.

When it comes to new patients, maybe they had a better or similar experience on their first call with another practice that could offer an appointment sooner. Maybe they just called on a whim and changed their mind before their visit. Something else could have pulled their finances away unexpectedly. Or as I mentioned, maybe it simply became inconvenient.

So what exactly defines a no-show? Some practices define no-shows simply as someone who didn't show up to their appointment. You may consider defining a no-show as someone who changes their appointment within twenty-four hours—when they call with such little prior notice that the appointment can't be backfilled, it's as good as a no-show from a productivity perspective. When looking at your office, instead of one global metric for no-show rates, consider separating out active patients from new patients, and then define a goal to reach for each one.

Regardless of the reason, no-show rates are higher for new patients because they've got no skin in the game. There's no natural consequence to them not showing up. Conversely, since we gave away that appointment, the consequences for us—for your practice—are very real. You may be able to fill that slot if you keep a wait list, but if not, you're going to have lost productivity time that could have been used for something better than just standing around waiting for a patient to show up.

For these reasons and more, we've got to have an extraordinary patient intake process. It must be polite, polished, professional. And it must continue to adapt as the world changes. At a time when disruptive businesses can sucker punch an entire industry (think Uber), we've got to continually adapt if we are to be the leader. As the Greek philosopher Heraclitus said: "There's nothing permanent except change."

Once your team understands the foundational components of the new patient call, they can be more comfortable adapting them to fit the personalities and situations they are dealing with. Because if the call doesn't go well and you don't get that patient in, you never get a chance to prove what a great journey and result you provide.

Thus far, we've been talking about the fun calls that lead up to the new patient call, along with tips for ensuring the new patient call goes well. But now we've got to flip the coin and look at the upset callers and other things that tend to get us in a bind. With the habits I've explained thus far, we hope to prevent these kinds of situations. But when they do occur, we also need to know how to fix them.

Huddle Up

- o **Are you taking new patient calls on paper or on the computer?**
- o **When was the last time you made any changes to your new patient intake sheet?**
- o **What's considered a no-show in your practice?**

Chapter 8

Upset Callers and Other Challenges

AN OUNCE OF PREVENTION IS WORTH A POUND OF CURE.

—BENJAMIN FRANKLIN

One of my clients had a practice in the Deep South. The office manager called me in because, as polite as the front desk team was, the practice still had more than its share of agitated patients. Especially on the phone but also in person, patients were sometimes so agitated that they would lash out at the front desk—sometimes, they left the front desk people in tears.

What I discovered during coaching was that all their natural southern charm actually offended the transplants to the area. Although the macroculture was "This is the South. We're all very friendly here," there was a microculture of people from other areas of the world. To those transplants, pouring on southern charm was a syrupy sweetness that was almost distasteful, and it had them pouncing on the front desk people.

We taught the front desk team to have a more businesslike tone in their voices. Instead of southern singsong, "Yes, ma'am," we taught them to say, "Yes, I would be glad to help you" or "I'd be happy to help you." Soon thereafter, unsolicited comments began pouring in from parents: "Wow, what have you done? The change in your team is amazing." No one realized the team had been through training, but the result was noticeable enough that people went out of their way to reach out to the office manager to let her know they now appreciated the front desk.

Perhaps the best news is that there were no more tears. Trained properly, the front desk now knows how to handle customers, no matter the situation. Through their businesslike tone, they are able to prevent many issues. And when any issue does arise, they're empowered with the know-how to take care of them.

The habits we've been talking about thus far are designed to help reduce the number of upset callers and upset patients. Things like first and last responses, treating people with politeness, understanding personalities, and wrapping the conversation in a beautiful presentation are helping to prevent upset callers from happening. At the same time, we're actually demonstrating to others how to treat us.

Unfortunately, even with all these habits, we will still have to deal with upset people every so often. One of the people I trained was a young woman who could handle the regular, go-as-they-should-go, or go-with-the-flow calls. But as soon as a call got a little tense, she kept trying to apply the same characteristics as the regular calls, and that made the people on the other end of the phone more agitated. When people are upset, we have to do something different. Making this adjustment takes a different skill set.

> When people are upset, we have to do something different.

The ALERT Method

You've likely heard of the abbreviations that various companies use for their customer recovery methods. Starbucks uses LATTE, which stands for listen, acknowledge, take action, thank, and explain (the latter of these, explain, is explaining back to their leaders what has happened). Marriott uses LEARN, which stands for listen, empathize, apologize, respond, notify—again letting somebody in leadership know. Very similar.

The one I like to use is ALERT: apologize/acknowledge, listen, empathize, resolve, and thank. I like this one because it's easy to remember, but it's also got just enough of an alarming tone that it makes us think, "Whoa, hold up. What do I need to do here?"

Let's look at each of the elements of ALERT in turn.

Apologize/Acknowledge

When people are upset or frustrated, start by giving an authentic apology because people don't want to just hear the word *sorry*. "I apologize that you had an experience that did not meet your expectations"—that's an apology. *Sorry*, on the other hand, is something we tell toddlers to do: "Tell them you're sorry." Even when kids say it, they don't mean it. When we use *sorry* on the phone, parenting ears automatically go, "Ugh." So we use the word *apologize*, and we apologize for an experience that didn't meet their expectations. That is something we can apologize for. That serves the purpose and helps to quiet what's going on.

Listen

The biggest error we tend to make when dealing with an upset customer is interrupting them. Don't interrupt. Just let the vent happen. Most of the time, it's not you. They've had a bad day. Somebody got in line in front of them at Starbucks, and you just happened to be downhill from there.

Think about those Instant Pot pressure cookers. They come with a warning to not open the lid before the steam and pressure have been released. The same principle applies when dealing with upset people. We listen and do not interrupt or else it's like putting your hand in front of that steam. You are going to get scalded. But once that steam dissipates, once the pressure resolves, you can safely take the lid off and enjoy your meal—you can safely move forward with conversation, no harm done.

Most of us at the front desk are females. What do we do when we have a bad day? We call a girlfriend and go blah, blah, blah. Once we finish, we go, "Thanks for letting me vent." Our wonderful friend who listened without saying a word, who has simply let us vent, is like the pressure valve on that Instant Pot.

So when it comes to upset callers, the key is to listen. Let the pressure release. They may simply need to get their frustration out, which is why we use the term *vent.*

Empathize

Once the pressure has been released, then we say something to demonstrate that we emphasize with the caller: "I can appreciate how you can feel that," or, "I can understand why that is frustrating." An empathetic response shows we heard them and we can relate.

Empathy is different and more impactful than sympathy. Sympathy expresses a level of sadness toward the other person's situation. It can even be mistaken for pity, especially to an upset caller. Empathy, on the other hand, demonstrates an immediate willingness to align on some level with the caller, acknowledging that you can understand what it's like to be in their shoes.

Resolve

When it comes to a resolution, we want to be sure we don't give the moon. However, here again, we're dealing with a fire scenario, and what does fire need? Options and authority, which means the ability to make a choice. In the same way we offer choices during the appointment setting, we offer a controlled set of choices when offering a resolution for an upset caller: "Mrs. Jones, let's see what we can do to make this right. We could do this, or we could do that. Which would you prefer?"

Now here is the thing: If we ever feel ourselves getting emotionally entangled in this, we need to punt. We need to pass this off to the office manager or someone else who can provide a resolution. "Mrs. Jones, I hear that this is not going as we intended. May I get Michelle to help us out with this?" Ask for their permission, and then pass it off. Don't do what I saw one front desk person do: when she reached the point of frustration, she just hung up the phone. Hanging up certainly does not make for a happy caller. We ourselves cannot be the problem.

> Hanging up certainly does not make for a happy caller. We ourselves cannot be the problem.

Thank

Finally, we want to thank the caller. In today's world of social media, where every interaction can be broadcast worldwide in seconds, we want to thank the caller for actually bringing the problem to our attention and giving us the opportunity to fix it. "Thank you for bringing this to my attention so we could get a solution. Thank you for giving me the opportunity to make this right for you. Is there anything else I can help you with today?"

ALERT is one more example of how small repeatable habits make all the difference. With ALERT, we have a real opportunity to turn upset people into raving fans. We can take them through a transition of feelings, from low to high, and then, as the Heath brothers explained in *The Power of Moments*, lock in a moment of truth. Together, ALERT habits have a synergistic effect that makes for better new patient calls, helps prevent upset callers, and can have a huge impact on your company.

Handling the Nonhappy

Sometimes, patients have problems that they want addressed. Many of the problems are simply nonhappy items, such as "my stitches hurt." But if we don't handle the call well and effectively, then what was merely a frustration can escalate into an upset caller. Depending on the situation, these calls must sometimes be pushed up the ladder, for instance, from the front desk to someone in the clinical area. However, that may not always be necessary.

When something has gone awry or there's an actual emergency, sometimes we're not even talking to the actual patient. We're playing the role of liaison. Let me use an example from the orthodontic world. The patient is a teenager at school who has texted their mom that there's a problem but has not really given a good description of what's wrong. The mom, now flustered, calls up your office. Now you or your administrative team are trying to interpret clinically what needs to happen. If the problem has happened on a Friday and the doctor is not in, does he or she need to be called?

This scenario is ripe for miscommunication about the actual need and solution. In fact, it can become a nightmare when trying to interpret a vague, third-party explanation of a problem for an office with multiple doctors and clinicians.

One way to prepare for nonhappy and emergency calls that come in is to create an if-then flowchart that stacks the various scenarios against the various solutions. An if-then flowchart can help prevent every nonhappy or "emergency" call from being pushed up the ladder.

Your if-then chart might cover the following scenarios:

- If this happens, then they need to be seen the same day.

- If this, then get them in the next day.

- If this, then notify the on-call doctor.

- If this, then they don't need to be seen right away, but we'll move up their next appointment.

- If this, then add extra time to their next appointment.

The if-then scenarios will be unique to your office. And the number of scenarios can multiply depending on the number of doctors and even clinicians in the practice. You can imagine how without procedures in place, this can be a communication nightmare.

Let me tell you about the solution implemented by one orthodontic office that I worked with. The front desk had a lot of new people at the time, most of whom were unsure about the if-then situations at the office. Without ready solutions, these newbies would put nonhappy and emergency callers on hold—sometimes making an already frustrated person wait for five or ten minutes. Talk about pissing somebody off! Now the person is not only frustrated by their problem but also upset with the way they're being handled.

The practice decided to adopt a model that many medical offices use. When an if-then call came in, the front desk would tell the caller that they were going to have the person handling such calls that day give them a call back within the hour. After that, the number of calls that were ten minutes or longer dropped by 64 percent! The front desk person was able to take the next call more effectively, and the person who has the emergency is talking to the person who's actually going to fix it for them. Now they're not turning frustrations into upsets.

When a caller is already frustrated, a front desk that is not empowered to handle the situation can muck it up worse. That can cause us to lose one more of those all-important connection points. Instead of playing the telephone game, where a caller gets passed on to someone who is a mismatch for resolving their problem, a flowchart and training can help callers be connected to the source who can fix their problem.

Sentences on the Phone, Paragraphs in Person

As I've been sharing throughout the book, we need a plan for our teams to follow that helps keep them from sounding like they're just spouting a lot of blah, blah, blah on the phone.

Implementing that plan includes understanding how to use the right words and share information in the appropriate format. If your team is uncomfortable with a topic, then they may default to verbal diarrhea on the subject, giving a rambling dissertation to try to justify the information.

The key is to remember that delivering information comes down to a simple rule: sentences on the phone, paragraphs in person.

When we're on the phone, we can't see the person on the other end of the line, but one thing is certain—their attention span is going to be even shorter than when they are in front of us. That's why I propose only providing details at sentence length when on the phone. Full education on the phone is confusing, tedious, and boring. We have to make the point or answer the question succinctly, then move on. It's like trying to educate someone via text—it's too complicated and may not get the point across.

In person is another matter. This is where explanations can expand into full paragraphs. When someone is standing right before us, we have the benefit of reading body language to assess if the message is landing effectively, and then we can adapt as necessary.

Aids for Complex Questions

The sentence/paragraph rule is especially important when it comes to complex questions. In fact, with certain conversations, we need to stay with an almost bullet point discussion, especially on the phone. For instance, "Do you take my insurance?"

"Yes, we do take insurances and file to maximize your benefits." We definitely don't want to run on at length: "Well, you see, orthodontic insurance is different from medical insurance, and you pay this, and you do that, and they pay you over time." We don't want to try to educate and explain very complex information on the phone.

Instead, when it comes to complex topics such as insurance, pay policies, appointment policies, and detailed instructions, visual aids and other tools can help provide clarity for your team—and your patients. These tools might include pictorial handouts, which can make it easier for your team to stay on topic while on the phone, or they can be used to provide patients with greater comprehension of very complex topics. When the patient comes in, they can be given the handout, which can be accompanied by paragraph-length explanations from the front desk.

When it comes to money questions, we try to simplify the complex by looking at the question behind the question. For instance, on a new patient call, questions about money are really about affordability. Answers like "Mrs. Jones, we have been very successful at making payment plans to fit monthly budgets" can help a person on the phone feel more comfortable about their decision.

Take a page out of the car commercials advertising book. They rarely talk about the big number. What they talk about is "payments as low as." The key is to not overemphasize the point. "Mrs. Jones, we have been successful in getting down payments as low as X and monthlies as low as X. Would that work for you?" Have a succinct answer, and then move on.

So far, I've given you a lot of information to use when working with patients, potential patients, and potential customers. This has only been a portion of what I share in my coaching and training sessions. In the next chapter, I will share some other advice about working with patients on the phone as the last part of the road map.

Huddle Up

- ○ **Who's the rock star in your office that can turn an upset person into a raving fan?**
- ○ **Do you have an if-then flowchart that stacks possible problems against the solutions?**

Are there any other complex topics that need a handout to help explain to patients who come into the office how, for example, insurance or payment plans work? You can read about these and more at my website, www.communicateexcellence.com.

Chapter 9

Connection Calls and Other Outbound Calls

THE MOST IMPORTANT THING IN COMMUNICATION IS HEARING WHAT ISN'T SAID.

—PETER DRUCKER

When I was homeschooling my three kids, we would go to the library every week. While the older two kids were allowed to look around the library and pick out books, my youngest, David, was around eighteen months old, so I would carry him in a backpack-style child carrier. Since he still wasn't talking at the time, I taught him some American Sign Language as a way of communicating. Often, while the other two were still looking around, David would get fidgety and begin signing "all done, all done" to let me know that he was ready to go home. I would then say back to him, "David, I understand you're all done and want to go. Jesse and Katy are picking out their last books, and then we'll go." At that point, he would relax. Even though he didn't use the right words, he had communicated with me. I acknowledged that I had heard him, acknowledged what he was trying to communicate to me, and told him the next step. That relaxed him because he knew he had gotten his point across.

Similarly, I have a kind of nonverbal communication with my golden retriever, Lucy. When we go out for a walk, if she's done, she puts on the brakes—dead stop. She doesn't say a word, but she's communicating to me, "I'm done. We're going home now." Other times, she lets me know when we get to the end of the block whether it's going to be a long walk or a short one—if she heads left, we're going on a short walk; right, it's going to be a long walk. She does not use words, but she knows how to communicate with me.

These are just two examples of what I mean when I say there is more to communication than just our words. Through our nonverbal communications, we can also demonstrate caring to patients, potential patients, and potential customers.

In this chapter, I'll explain why this concept is important on two other types of calls: confirmation calls and other outbound calls.

Connection Calls

What are typically known as "confirmation calls" I refer to as "connection calls." Why? Because with these types of calls, the connection is sometimes made by what we *don't* say.

We have all experienced this scenario: thanks to caller ID, we let the answering machine or our voicemail answer the call. After all, it's only a confirmation call from our doctor reminding us that we have an appointment or an obligation. These days, for current patients, the calls are sometimes automated. When it's a new patient, however, our front desk team may actually pick up the phone and make the call. Either way, it usually goes something like this: "I'm calling to confirm your appointment for tomorrow at such and such time."

We have a love-hate relationship with these ritualistic confirmation calls. On the one hand, we appreciate a reminder of our upcoming appointment in case we did not write it down correctly. On the other hand, once we begin hearing the details, we hit "delete." Rarely does anyone receiving such a call listen to the full message, in part because the usual confirmation call barely hovers above the level of mediocrity. We know what they're going to say, so we give it a quick listen, delete it, and then get on with our day.

The question then is this: why do we think we are doing something different by simply having a live voice instead of an automated voice do the same thing?

If we want to be different from the usual confirmation call, then we need to change the purpose from merely confirming and reminding the patient to connecting with them and drawing on the authority of our doctors. We can let patients know we are anticipating and preparing for their visit.

With new patients, this goal is easy to accomplish by referencing the status of their new patient forms. By using the connection call as an opportunity to thank or remind the caller about the forms, we demonstrate that we have taken an early initiative in preparing for their visit. The purpose is not just to remind them to fill out their forms if they have not already done so. It is actually personalizing the message to them.

Of course, to personalize the call, we need to first review the patient details to see if they have filled out their forms. If so, then the call will involve a thank-you. Conversely, if the items are not yet submitted, then the call will include a reminder. With either version, we want to draw on the authority of the doctor and use Cialdini's principles of persuasion (see chapter 3).

Here is a sample call for a new patient who has completed their forms.

Good evening, this is Mary from Dr. Smile's office.

Dr. Smile reviewed your records and, seeing that you have completed them, asked me to personally thank you for having done so. We are looking forward to meeting everyone.

Again, this is Mary, and I will be at the front desk to meet you when you come in for your consultation tomorrow at eight o'clock. If you have any questions before then, please call or text me at 555.555.5555.

Have a great day!

Here is a sample call to someone who has not completed their forms.

Good evening, this is Mary from Dr. Smile's office.

As Dr. Smile was reviewing your records, she noticed that the new patient forms were still not in our system and asked me to ensure you still had the appropriate link to those forms. After this call, I will resend you the link via the e-mail we have for you. Additionally, the online forms are located on our website at www.communicateexcellence.com.

If you are unable to submit those tonight, Dr. Smile requests you arrive fifteen minutes early so you have time to complete those forms and ensure all the details are prepared in advance of your one-on-one time with the doctor. We are looking forward to meeting everyone.

Again, this is Mary, and I will be at the front desk to meet you when you come in for your consultation tomorrow morning at eight o'clock. Should you have any questions before then, please call or text me at 555.555.5555.

Have a great day!

Both examples demonstrate that we have taken the time to prepare and anticipate their visit. By turning the confirmation call into a connection call, we're communicating that we're paying attention to this new patient without actually saying those very words. That action may help to keep the patient engaged longer.

In this age, we're competing for discretionary income; people who have choices expect more than mediocre. If we're mediocre, and we're the third consult in the line, they may go with number two and never give us a chance simply because number two offers a little bit of a deal.

If we're excellent, especially from the first call and then all the way through the journey, they'll wait to make sure they come in to see us. If we continue to be excellent from the first contact, as opposed to being mediocre, they will tell others about us as well.

> By turning the confirmation call into a connection call, we're communicating that we're paying attention to this new patient without actually saying those very words.

Outbound Calls Are Just As Important

While most offices usually do some form of training for the inbound call, many offices fail to train staff on outbound calls. Aside from confirming appointments, the reasons for outbound calls vary; often, we make them to try to get new patients back on the books. That's just one reason why the outbound call is just as important as the inbound call.

Here are some of the best practices for these calls.

An Authentic but Scripted Greeting

When it comes to outbound calls, the greeting isn't like our everyday greeting, but it must still demonstrate excellence. Often, with an outbound call, the intended recipient is not the person who answers the phone. In order to keep the person answering the phone from feeling like they're getting caught in a gotcha moment, we don't start by asking "Mrs. Jones?" Instead, we first introduce ourselves: "Good morning, this is Amy from Company XYZ. May I please speak with Mrs. Jones?" We start with a full greeting so they don't feel like they're getting tricked into a conversation.

This greeting is so important that you may want to write it into the script. The goal is to be intentional and authentic up front—this is who I am and where I'm from.

Use the Caller's or Patient's Name

Another way that demonstrates we care is to use the person's name. That doesn't mean that we're trying to hit a certain number of instances. "Mrs. Jones this. Mrs. Jones that," as if we have to say it three times before we get our gold star. It means naturally trying to find times to use their name because science shows that our brain is triggered by hearing our own name.

Scientists have wired people up and systematically read names at a certain rate. Anytime a person's name was said, even if it was in the middle of a list, their brain lit up. We might as well use that connection to help lock in one of those moments of truth.[5]

---

5   Dennis P. Carmody and Michael Lewis, "Brain Activation When Hearing One's Own and Others' Names," *Brain Research* 1116, no. 1 (October 20, 2006): 153–158, accessed August 10, 2019, on PMC, https://www.ncbi.nlm.nih.gov/pmc/articles/PMC1647299/.

Use the person's name naturally. At the beginning of the call, we ask, "May I have your name?" Then we ask, "Mrs. Jones, what's your child's name?" And that continues throughout the call. Then at the end of the call, we say, "Mrs. Jones, I hope you have a great day." It's like using spice. Pepper the name lightly throughout the conversation, but don't pour it on. A little enhances, too much ruins.

Be Responsive

Responding to any additional information the caller provides demonstrates caring. If they say, "I'm calling to reschedule because my son is sick," we say, "I'm sorry to hear that. Is he doing okay?" By listening, being curious, and asking one more question, we show a level of responsiveness and empathy that cannot be scripted.

> Pepper the name lightly throughout the conversation, but don't pour it on. A little enhances, too much ruins.

Being responsive is about picking up a tidbit and repeating it back. Maybe we heard about Johnny's illness on the call, or maybe we heard, "We're going on vacation." At the end of the call, instead of, "Have a great day," we might say, "I hope Johnny feels better tomorrow" or "I hope you enjoy your vacation." Again, it's about responsiveness.

I've thrown a lot at you in the previous chapters, covering some of what I would work through with your team members as a communications coach.

In the last part of the book, I will share with you tips for implementing a plan on your own. If you consider that as an option, then remember, as you go through these lessons, excellence is a journey, not a destination.

Huddle Up

○ Do any of the scenarios that I've included in this part of the book—the new patient, the upset caller—require a checklist within your own practice to make sure that you're communicating within the team in an effective way?

○ Who on your team is designated to check the status of any submission forms?

○ Have you made it easy for new patients to turn in forms ahead of time?

Part III

Communicate Excellence

With the information I shared in part two of this book, you now have some tools and insights to plan and implement your own training program.

But there are challenges when implementing a plan to communicate excellence on your own amid the chaos of running your own business.

In this section of the book, I'm going to help you see why you have to continue to lead and continue to work on this training. It's not a one-and-done kind of process. I will also share with you some of the reasons to consider hiring a coach to work the plan.

Chapter 10

Continue to Lead

TO HANDLE YOURSELF, USE YOUR HEAD; TO HANDLE OTHERS, USE YOUR HEART.

—ELEANOR ROOSEVELT

In orthodontics, creating a great smile is about moving teeth into a new position, while plastic surgery is about reshaping or rejuvenating the body either into a new form or a refreshed look.

With orthodontics or plastic surgery, the outcomes can also often rely on forming new habits posttreatment. With teeth, for instance, a retainer must be worn or they will have a tendency to shift back to where they were before the braces or aligners. With plastic surgery, better self-care can help prolong results that will naturally be impacted by aging and environment and other factors over time.

In some ways, both of these examples are very much like the coaching and training your team will undergo. What starts as an individual with an imperfect presentation then becomes a more polished and professional team member after coaching and training. But building and maintaining their new habits is all about consistency. You've got to keep coaching because we are constantly feeling that pull back to our old habits. Just like teeth can gravitate back toward their original positions and a reshaped body can experience the constant pull of gravity and the impact of aging, new communication habits can become lax if they are not continually addressed through maintenance coaching and training.

The effort you put into forging new habits will reward you and your team in performance posttraining. However, the truth is that you can never really stop working on communicating excellence.

Not One-and-Done

Once your team has completed initial coaching, they need to continue in maintenance mode. Building new habits is not a one-and-done process. Here are some reasons you have to keep working on them.

Flipping the switch. When it comes to communication in the business, sometimes the lines of demarcation are not as clear. Unlike a doctor or clinical assistant or salesperson who can more or less flip a switch and turn on their medical or sales skills, it can be more difficult to flip that switch when in a front desk role because the communication skills are so similar to what we use every day. All day long, we communicate with our family and our friends, so switching gears is a little harder because the line is not always distinct. Am I talking to a friend now? Am I talking to a customer? Since we use communication all day long, those everyday communication habits are always tugging at your front desk people, trying to blur the lines and pull them away out of front desk mode. It's not the same as being able to lay down the scalpel, pliers, or sales presentation and go home.

Fast pace of change. Another reason we have to keep working on habits is because our audience keeps changing and the pace of that change keeps increasing. Twenty or thirty years ago, when we had more stay-at-home moms, the pace of change of our intended audience was much slower. Today, we're in a rapid-pace environment, where our intended audience is continually distracted by new products, new ways of delivering service, new ways of doing things. We have to keep adapting our communication methods.

Filling in the gap. As I've stated, many front desk people are in their first real job. Up to now, communication has largely been using text to talk to friends. They've not had a leader show them how to communicate in a professional environment—all they've known is the text world, and they may not have even spent much time talking on the phone.

Then there are the older workers who have been behind a desk for decades but have never seen anything like the pace of technological change we're seeing today. It's easy for them to fall back into thinking, "That's the way we've always done it."

With either of these types of workers, you risk having patients and potential patients falling through the gaps. If we bring the two ends of the communication spectrum closer together, then we can close the gap that is letting patients and potential patients slip through. If we don't pay attention to it, that gap could become a chasm. We've got to help the younger ones refine their language, and we've got to help the older ones adapt their language.

> We've got to help the younger ones refine their language, and we've got to help the older ones adapt their language.

It can be a lot for a busy clinical professional to continually lead, to hold regular coaching sessions with your team. In fact, the training itself can sometimes increase the stress of an already busy office. The key is to keep everything in balance.

There Will Be Challenges

Surges of stress from fluctuating workloads or other factors can make it hard to work on changing habits. Your office volume likely has peaks and valleys. While the early months of the year might be busier for plastic surgeons as their patients get ready for summer and swimsuit season, for orthodontists, summer months—when school is out—tend to be the most chaotic. And August can bring triple the business when all parents want their kids in braces before school begins. Then when schools starts, the silence of the office means you hear crickets. With team members on vacation during the summer months, you may be staffing at 80 percent volume when you've got 200 percent volume. Even though the cycle tends to happen year after year, it's still difficult to be prepared. We either increase staff or really rally around all that volume.

There are other kinds of stress as well: staff turnover or illness, someone bringing troubles from home into the office. All this can impact performance—just when you're trying to hone your team.

We all know that we need a certain amount of stress in order to perform well. But if we tip that stress too far, performance falls off. Not enough stress and boredom sets in; too much stress and unhappiness and anxiety set in.

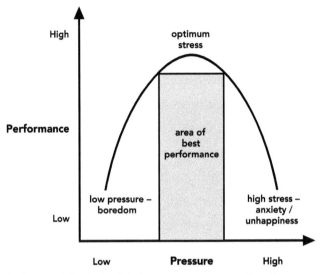

The Inverted-U relationship between pressure and performance

Fig. 10.1. The Inverted-U Curve

The model in figure 10.1 shows what is known as the Yerkes-Dodson Law, or the Inverted-U Curve. As you can see by the rectangle in the model, optimal performance is gained when the pressure or the stress is neither too low nor too high.

So the thing to do is to find that ideal stress zone. We don't want boredom to set in, yet we don't want to burn out our team members either.

Here's the thing. Stress, and consequently the U curve, can actually shift. When we master a skill involving a certain task, that task becomes easier to us. It doesn't seem as complex, and we can handle more stress before our performance falls off. Conversely, if we have not mastered a skill involving a certain task, then that task seems much harder for us. When we haven't learned a habit and really locked it in, it doesn't take much stress before we are knocked off our game.

With coaching skills and drills, we can lock in the curve—we can keep the rectangle in an optimum place. Think of Michael Jordan. He was well known for being at practice before everyone else and staying until after everyone left. He wanted to make sure he mastered those shots so that when the pressure was high, he could say, "Give me the ball. I can make that shot."

Now, if the stress levels get too high, for whatever reason, our people can go into survival mode. In survival mode, performance falls off. But by making sure our team members have a mastery of skills, we can ensure our team can handle more stress before their performance begins to deteriorate.

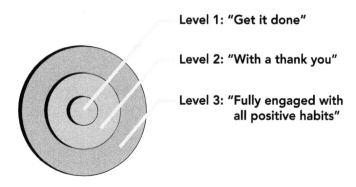

Level 1: "Get it done"

Level 2: "With a thank you"

Level 3: "Fully engaged with all positive habits"

Fig. 10.2. Survival mode circles

Let me illustrate this idea using the rings and circles in figure 10.2. As you can see, at level one—the innermost circle—you find the bare-bones, basic, get-it-done skills. These are the "Yeah. Hi. Bye. Whatever, see you later" kinds of conversations you might hear.

As we get more mastery of skills and improved habits, we may improve two pieces of common courtesy: "Yes, thank you. Oh, you're welcome. May I do this?" This is the level two ring.

But what we want to aim for is the outermost ring, level three. We want fully engaged, proficient, and positive habits. That way, even if there is a slight slippage, it may only be back to level two, which is still very polite.

So train to that level three mastery but also be aware of what stress does to your performance. That's the trick—to find the sweet spot where you can insert training effectively *even while* running a busy office. Be aware so you can recognize the signs that you've pushed your team too far, which typically happens because the workload is so high, the training is too intense, or the team member is not capable of handling the expected work—or a combination of these.

If you suspect that might be happening, then look for some key performance indicators (KPIs) that might indicate you're hitting the downward part of the curve. Some of these KPIs might be:

- **Lengthier calls.** A surge in calls going longer than ten minutes can be a sign that your team is placing people on hold more often.

- **More calls starting with an immediate hold.** This often means that your front desk person has somebody standing in front of them, they're already on the phone, and the phone rings again. They've got to do something with that incoming call, so they pick it up and immediately put the caller on hold.

- **More frustrated callers.** Are you or your office manager getting more calls passed to you?

- **Negative energy.** Are you starting to feel a sense of frustration and energy within your office?

- **Less politeness.** If you stop and listen to one or two calls, do you like what you're hearing? Do your team members seem to be a little shorter with callers, giving quick, less polite answers?

All these things may be indicating that the stress is getting too high and the performance is falling off.

On the other hand, there are also indicators that we're making progress. Let's look at a few of those.

Signs of Progress

Sometimes, we become so acclimated to our surroundings that we fail to see things for what they really are. That happens in our offices—we really find it impossible to understand our patients' perspectives.

Even though you can never truly experience what it's like to be a first-time visitor to your office, try to put yourself in those shoes for a moment—what do you notice? What's the energy like in the office? What's the tone you're hearing in the voices? What do you notice even if all you hear is one side of a conversation?

There are some signs that you, as a leader, can identify to help you recognize when your team is progressing:

- **Level three habits being used.** By listening to recordings of your team on the phone, you can begin to hear when the habits they're learning are actually being used.

- **Fewer upset callers.** Finding fewer notes on your desk along the lines of "You've got to call this mom back" is a sign your coaching is working.

- **Improved call metrics.** If you have a system that collects data on your calls, you should be able to tell by your call length numbers whether your team members are implementing new habits. The length of the calls should be decreasing because they are putting fewer people on hold. Such a system can help you identify progress without even having to listen to calls.

- **Lower no-show rates.** If your appointments are being made more effectively, you should notice a decrease in your no-show rates.

- **Growing feeling of confidence.** When your team is progressing, frustration and stress levels will lower, contentment levels will rise, and confidence will improve. You'll start to see your team working more like a well-oiled machine, and you'll start to feel the positive energy.

Above all, remember that excellence is not a destination, it's a journey, and you have to continue to work on it.

Plan for Peak Performance

Yes, you are busy. But, whether you're a small business or a large business, you've got to take time for training. Take a lesson from sports teams—they are masters of this process. They follow the three Ps for peak performance, a concept developed by Jack Daly but which I've adapted: execute according to a playbook, practice regularly, and have a professional coach. Let's look at how a plan for peak performance breaks down.

> Above all, remember that excellence is not a destination, it's a journey, and you have to continue to work on it.

Execute According to a Playbook

It is not enough to tell your team to "Just do your best." That's leaving a lot to chance. Professional athletes and teams have intentional habits, plays, and routines. Processes and systems are the building blocks of the playbooks for offices. With them, anyone can be trained efficiently and to a standard. They also keep you from being out of luck when a team member is out or moves on.

Practice Regularly

You know the saying "Practice makes perfect." Another is "We do not rise to the occasion; we fall back on our training." Then why do we fail to schedule practice time? Do you think a sports team would go through a season only playing games without practicing in between? No way!

Practice consumes well over 90 percent of the athlete's time. During the active season, an NBA (National Basketball Association) player may have three games a week but have a sixty-hour workweek. The three hours of regulation time on the court is a mere 5 percent of their workweek.

Of course, there's no way you can expect to have the same ratio of practice to game time, but what if we simply did the opposite proportion? What if we practiced 5 percent of the time? For a forty-hour workweek, that is two hours. Break that down further, and it is about twenty-five minutes per workday.

Schedule this time. Sharpen the saw. Run through scenarios. Never be caught off guard. Be intentional.

Have a Professional Coach

Athletic teams would never consider entering the "fields of friendly strife" without having a coach. Think of athletes, top performers, and teams. On many teams, there are numerous coaches or trainers, each with their own specialty. Your business teams are the same way. Your clinicians and administrative team members do not use the same skills to perform their duties.

So what does a coach do for your team? We're going to go into this in depth in the next chapter, but as quick introduction, a coach/consultant provides continuous and consistent accountability, guidance, and broader insights than you can on your own. A coach also provides a neutral observation vantage point. They are not so close or emotionally sucked in and can extract themselves from internal bias. How many of you don't mind training your peers but cringe at the thought of helping your kid with their homework? You may be great as a clinician, you may be great at training your team on those skills, maybe you even go out and train your peers. But training your front desk on customer service requires something of an emotional detachment to be done effectively. More than the time and energy involved, you're potentially in danger of disrupting the valuable environment of trust in your office—no one wants the boss to be peering over their shoulder all the time.

Plus, as an orthodontist or plastic surgeon, it's difficult to truly put yourself in your receptionists' shoes to teach them all they need to know. As someone in a position of authority, your patients and customers will always respond to you differently than they will to your front desk team. I've been there: I've seen patients treat me with a little more coldness that immediately melts once the doctor enters the picture—they immediately warm up at the sight of that white coat. I mentioned this earlier as the white coat syndrome; if the doctor says so, then it's all good.

The next time your front desk says, "You don't know what it's like," consider this: as the doctor or leader of your practice, there is no way you can truly know what it's like to be in their shoes.

We all know front desk work needs to be done, but for it to be done consistently and systematically, why not hire a coach? There is nobody else who can be the doctor but you, but you can sure delegate some things to others. Bringing in a coach to create a bespoke plan based on behaviors observed is an invaluable resource. Why not hire someone who has the skill set to help your team succeed—and to let you get back to doing the thing that only you can do?

Huddle Up

- ○ Do you have a training guide or playbook to help your front desk team improve their skills?
- ○ Have you ever listened to the recordings of your front desk calls?
- ○ Do you have dedicated training and practice time for your team members?
- ○ If you were actually to implement a plan on your own, have you thought through what's involved and who would be in charge of it? Are you going to pull away someone who is already at full capacity?

Chapter 11

Consider a Coach

IF YOU DON'T HAVE TIME TO DO IT RIGHT, WHEN WILL YOU HAVE TIME TO DO IT OVER?

—COACH JOHN WOODEN

Let me tell you about Debbie and her turnaround. Debbie was a member of a front desk team. She was a kind and sweet person. In fact, people often mistook her sweetness for mousiness, and they would, for lack of a better word, almost bully her.

We were working on repeatable habits that she could use in her role. It was our third month together, and I was preparing for her upcoming coaching session by listening to her recent reception recordings when, all of a sudden, we reached the tipping point. Finally, she got it. I thought I was hearing a new person. She went from being almost a mousy person to being a polite, guiding person in control. She went from "Well, do you want to come in at this time?" to "Yes, so what we have available is this or this."

Whoa. What happened?

> She went from being almost a mousy person to being a polite, guiding person in control.

The coaching feedback loop and her efforts had made all the difference. When I shared with her that there was a recognizable change, that she sounded like a whole new person, she said, "Thank you. I'm not so nervous coming in to work now. I'm not fearful of those callers." She just feels so much more confident in her role.

A Three-Phase Approach

Good coaching includes having a standardized and repeatable plan. It requires being committed to setting aside consistent time for training. It means being able to provide feedback without bias. Are you ready to do these things? Or is it time to consider bringing in someone who is trained to be a coach?

I take a three-phase approach to coaching.

Phase one—initial training. This phase involves a general introduction to this process and begins putting tools in your team members' toolboxes. In this phase, I lay the foundation for what's to come.

Phase two—apprenticeship coaching. I call this phase the Quick Start to Your Success. It involves rapid-succession coaching and feedback iteration to establish and change habits. There is enough time in between sessions to see progress, but the sessions are not so far apart that we lose momentum.

The goal is to help every team member build repeatable habits that have the greatest impact on your team and your practice.

Phase three—maintenance coaching. After habits have been established, we enter the third phase, which is maintenance coaching. That's how we help you and your team sustain your success.

This phase is customized and adapted to your various employees. For those who need a little more coaching, the sessions might be closer together. For rock stars, maybe a little further apart.

The goal is to help every team member build repeatable habits that have the greatest impact on your team and your practice.

A Winning Coach

There is something special about certain coaches. Some know how to win no matter who is on their team. They know how to draw the best out of every player. Remember the St. Louis Blues hockey team's 2018–19 season? In January, they were in last place. But at the end of the season, they took home the Stanley Cup. What changed? Their coach.

There are some ways to spot a winning coach to help your team build the repeatable habits you need to win. Here are a few questions to consider asking in advance.

What is your coaching background? Make sure the coach you're considering has a tried-and-true system for coaching your team to success.

Have you been trained on how to develop a structured plan? Has the coach undergone any special training or received any certifications that demonstrate communication excellence?

Have you ever written curriculum? Does the coach have an educational background, one that required them to make and execute plans?

What kind of successes have you demonstrated? How many clients have they coached to success?

Have you ever worked a front desk? Does the coach you're considering know what it's like to be behind the front desk?

Have you ever been in a role that required you to answer the phones and provide customer service? What kinds of roles has the coach been in that lend themselves to being in your team's shoes?

Have you worked in the business world as well? Do they have a résumé that includes roles in small businesses or corporations?

Have you been recognized for your ability to provide feedback? Ask the coach for testimonials that speak to their ability to provide constructive feedback that produces results.

Does your coaching program include listening to recordings? Most coaching involves only the occasional mystery call. But the best feedback comes from listening to recordings of calls and then providing honest encouragement and steps for success.

Do you tailor training to my team? It's important to know if the coaching is a one-size-fits-all plan or if it will be tailored to the needs of individual team members.

Do you provide follow-up? What kind of reinforcement does the coach provide? Is there, for instance, an e-mail after each session containing notes and clips of recordings, as well as some comments or ways to look back at the lesson for greater reinforcement?

Do you do drills and skills? What are the coach's methods for closing the gap between observable behavior and desired behavior?

At Communicate Excellence, we provide training and coaching to ensure the experience your team receives is positively memorable. We want your team to communicate excellence so consumers never consider going anywhere else.

I want your team members to be as memorable as Tracy. Remember my experience with her that I shared at the beginning of the book? Although she worked for a relatively forgettable, very large practice, I'll never forget the lasting impact she made on me and my family. She was so impactful that all these years later, it's helped shape the program I now use to coach and train others. Her legacy reached beyond the walls of the business, and I want your team members to make such a lasting impression that it will have the same kind of ripple effects.

With coaching, you can have a team of Tracys.

Huddle Up

Which of these is your office?

A) **We have first-call resolution for 80 percent of calls.**

B) **Our callers are on hold an average of ten minutes.**

A) **We have a standardized way of communicating.**

B) **Our team basically goes rogue when it comes to communicating.**

A) **Every caller gets the same experience no matter who answers the phone.**

B) **We have a good cop, bad cop kind of team.**

A) **Our office manager spends a disproportionate amount of their time fielding complaints.**

B) **Our office manager stays busy doing the job she was hired to do—manage the office.**

A) **Every day, I spend the last hour or more giving callbacks to angry patients/parents.**

B) **Every day, I spend the last few minutes reading through some of the great comments we're getting about our front desk team.**

A) **I'm constantly interrupted by my front desk team with questions about what I think should be their jobs.**

B) **I haven't had to answer questions about how to handle the front desk in months.**

If you answered A more than B, it might be time to consider hiring a coach. Reach out to me at www.communicateexcellence.com.

Conclusion

Work the Plan

IF YOU FAIL TO PLAN, YOU ARE PLANNING TO FAIL.

—BENJAMIN FRANKLIN

Everything that I've shared with you in this book works but only if it's executed. In other words, the plan works if you work the plan.

That plan is a road map that includes training and coaching in proven business principles. It includes helping your team members understand how to be polite and courteous without being pushovers. It includes team members learning the types of questions to use in their dance of conversation with patients, potential patients, and potential customers. And it includes using a personality assessment to better understand where we and others are coming from. All of these are then used to help team members learn how to open and close conversations, talk to new patients, reduce no-show rates, and schedule appointments to minimize peaks and valleys and keep your practice running smoothly. Of course, they need to know how to deal with upset patients and customers whether on the phone or in person.

When it comes to a communications plan, the coaching process and methodology can make all the difference in the outcome. There's more to coaching than just teaching. It must include follow-through and accountability to turn knowledge into action. It must include observing actions and providing feedback. It must include guiding your team through repeatable habits to help them learn how to foster the environment of a good experience.

The working of habits is not an event; it's a process. And coaching is a continuation of that process. Simply loading up your team's toolbox with tools doesn't mean they will know how to use them. There must be an apprenticeship component to it. That's why my coaching involves having your people watch me use the tool before I watch them use the tool and give them feedback on how they're using it. That's what makes this process work. That's what keeps you from going from book to book and consultant to consultant looking for the next magic bullet.

> The working of habits is not an event; it's a process.

As part of my coaching, I listen to over ten thousand calls every year. And some of what I've heard on those calls—before coaching—would dismay those providers that I'm working for. But I've found that by listening to those calls and then helping the team member learn certain repeatable habits in a consistent fashion, they are able to elevate every conversation. They don't ramble or leave out critical details. Bit by bit, one or two habits at a time, your team members become empowered to relate to people on a professional level every minute of every working day.

Once your team is presenting a standardized, consistent impression, you'll feel the energy in your practice change. No more tension or negative vibes. You'll find that there's a spirit of unity, of pride in their work. You'll find yourself with a team that is working together to authentically put the needs of the customer first. A team that knows how to handle oops moments with resolutions, not excuses.

The front desk is not an easy job. It's not easy being onstage all day. But when your team members are empowered to communicate excellence, they turn customers into raving fans who will do some of your marketing footwork for you. Your practice will become the one that people turn to versus everyone else in the market.

In today's world of direct-to-consumer options, there are still plenty of people who want to be treated special. Whether it's an adult paying for their own treatment or a parent paying for their child, they are buying more than a clinical product or service from you. They're buying an experience—what they expect will be an exceptional journey.

That journey is exceptional when it's congruent. If you are a high-end service, you need to be high-end everywhere. You don't want to be thought of as just a transaction. That makes you a commodity. The easiest and best way to demonstrate that you aren't either of those is through the service and treatment you provide your customers. The one, two, or three degrees of difference in the environment created by your team add up until you reach that boiling point where you have the steam you need to power the locomotive.

> If you are a high-end service, you need to be high-end everywhere.

The next magic bullet for communicating excellence doesn't happen simply by gaining more knowledge. It's the application of that knowledge that gives you the win. It's like a diet plan. You can read about plans all day long, but until you actually execute what you read, you won't lose weight, you won't improve your health, and you won't enjoy the journey to a better you. It's the same for your patients and potential patients and customers.

You're a specialist in your field, but you're not a communication specialist. Let us help you train, coach, and empower your staff to start more patients. Remember: we've got to grab them at hello, or you'll be telling them goodbye.

Acknowledgments

Write a book.

So easy to put on a bucket list yet so laborious to execute. I imagined my first book to be about a different topic, but like the whole of my life, circumstances and opportunities change. So you take each next right step and see where it leads you. I encourage you to do the same.

My path to writing *Communicate Excellence* came about because of many people. They nurtured me, consoled me, fought for me, taught me, corrected me. They provided insights and opportunities. I am forever grateful.

To my teachers at Faith Christian School, Hazelwood West High School, the United States Military Academy, Missouri University of Science and Technology, and the University of Phoenix. I thank you for all the lessons you provided.

To West Overland Bible Church, for the many wonderful years there with Awana and church camp. Pastor Meyer, you are so special.

To my children. Oh, how I loved seeing your eyes dance and minds open as we homeschooled. You taught me to see through innocent eyes and to love learning every day.

To long-standing friends. Andy and Katie. Rick and Jennifer. Elise. From homeschool, church, and baseball, we have been through ups and downs, yet we press onward.

To Michelle Dickerson. Without you and Nikki fighting on my behalf, I would have never started over.

To Len Botkin. We go way back. From high school to West Point to Bank of America. Thank you for helping me navigate my return to the workforce and helping me return to "the girl you knew back in high school" who had drive and confidence.

To Becky Johnson, Ann Starrette, Nicole Greer, and Shari Breandel. You saw a diamond in the rough and nurtured me when I was lower than low. You dressed me up, set me up, got me stable, and sent me out.

To Stonebridge Church Community and its members. Thank you for supporting me and teaching me. There has been no other church like you. You have incredible music and pastors. Thank you, Pastor Rick, for fulfilling my wish to start my wedding to Don with the line from *The Princess Bride:* "Mawwage is what bwings us together today." And to Gwen Smith and Carrie Marshall, thank you for singing at my wedding.

To my coworkers and their families. Dan Bohen and Bill Sanders … oh, the days of CADA at Bank of America. We had each other's backs. Cindy and Keri, thank you for the times you hosted all of us at your houses. I have never had coworkers like any of you. Let's get out on the water again.

To Don. Your kindness and tenderness are beyond words. Without the opportunities you provided, none of this would have been possible. And by marriage you provided me two beautiful bonus daughters.

To my family. Clay and Mandy, I love you dearly. You are the best brother and sister. Mom, I sure miss Dad. He was so tender and kind. Thank you for sharing his life in *The Birthing Room.* And then, Ron. You joined our family and have been Papa to my kids. Thank you for all the times you helped us out! And to my aunts, uncles, and cousins. We are so fortunate to have had grandparents who upheld us in daily prayer.

To new dear friends. Al and Kathy. Bill and Dina. The "monthly" supper group. Thank you for making the transition to a new home so blessed. Marilyn, thank you for all you do to help. And Sue. Thank you for the walks and talks we have enjoyed. Finally, Betsy. You are so great. I love having another Midwestern transplant.

To the Schulman Group. To the many dear friends who allowed me to listen in on all you had to share. Wow. What an amazing group. And to the dear, dear friends who have loved and supported us along the way.

To my consultant colleagues. Thank you for letting me sit and soak under your knowledge and wisdom. You have provided so much blood, sweat, and tears to the profession. And you have taught well. I pray I was a good student. To Tina Byrne, thank you for the crash course before I had my first day at Don's office. To Rita Bauer, thank you for cheering me on and getting me out on the speaking circuit even after the adventure of mine that nearly shut down Toronto's airport … LOL. Thank you to you all for letting me stand with you.

To Mary Beth Kirkpatrick, Ryan Moynihan, and all at Gaidge and Impact360. Thank you for letting me pal around with you … even if once I left you at AAO 2018 I then fell and dislocated my shoulder. We make for some great stories.

To John McGill and Chris Bentson. You are incredible leaders in the field, and Don and I both thank you for all the advice and wisdom you have shared with us.

To Amy Schmidt and all the gang at Ortho2. What an incredible software that made my learning simplified as I was thrust into the orthodontic arena. I thank you for the opportunity to be part of the developer meetings and the Cutting Edge Webinars.

To Dr. Dave Paquette. Who knew those many years ago while Katy was getting treated in the early 2000s that our paths would grow from us being an orthodontist and a patient's mom to colleagues within the same field. Thank you to you and Jenny for all your amazing kindness.

To Team Demas Orthodontics. You have been my testing ground and beta testers. I have learned so much from you. Thank you for your patience and willingness.

Finally, to Dr. Ron Redmond. Thank you for allowing me to fill in at a Schulman Group TC meeting and speak. It was something I had on my bucket list and had a great time doing so. And for the kindness, love, and wisdom you and Margaret have shown, I thank you from the bottom of my heart.

About the Author

Amy Demas is the founder and president of Communicate Excellence, which provides standardized training for administrative and front office teams. While teaching is in Amy's DNA, her diverse background also gives her insight into what it means to succeed in the business world.

Amy was one of the first one thousand women to attend the United States Military Academy before earning a degree in mechanical engineering from the Missouri University of Science and Technology and later a master's degree in business administration and management from the University of Phoenix.

As a teacher, Amy homeschooled her three children to top-fifth-percentile results with the Duke University Talent Identification Program, earning not only state-level but national-level awards.

In business, Amy developed a pipe stress technology analysis handbook for petrochemical piping systems and would later work in process design at Bank of America, where she earned more than fifty-five US patents. She is still one of the most prolific inventors in the company's history. While there, she was awarded the title of Bank of America Inventor of the Year in 2009. At the bank she also earned her Six Sigma Green Belt certification.

Amy has also served in numerous leadership roles at Toastmasters—a worldwide organization that promotes communication and public speaking skills—and has earned the highest distinction of a Distinguished Toastmaster. She has been awarded numerous titles for her skills of speech evaluation. And each time she has served as a president of a club or governor of an area, she has led it to the highest award of distinction.

As a trainer and coach, Amy's mission is to uncover truths and use those insights to empower others.

www.ingramcontent.com/pod-product-compliance
Lightning Source LLC
Jackson TN
JSHW011939131224
75386JS00041B/1457